To Rev. & Mrs Moses Gitlin

in memory
of
the Author
by his daughters

Eugenia J. Abramous

E. Vick

Mary Slort

Los Angeles, CA.
6. 7. 67

THE
VARIOUS
MANIFESTATIONS
OF THE DEITY

THE VARIOUS MANIFESTATIONS OF THE DEITY

by Dr. Leon Rosenberg

૭

AMERICAN EUROPEAN BETHEL MISSION

252 No. Dillon • Los Angeles, California

THE VARIOUS MANIFESTATIONS OF THE DEITY

TABLE OF CONTENTS

PREFACE

The subject now before us for discussion, viz. "The Various Manifestations of the Deity," has been a matter of serious concern to the author. Many questions came up in his mind while he was still under rabbinical influence, which likewise troubled some of his colleagues in the Seminary.

Two of those questions were: "Why does the Bible speak of such manifold manifestations of God?" and "Why does the Bible use similar terms for pagan idols as it uses for the Living Eternal One?"

Although his searching of the Scriptures resulted in his acceptance of Jesus of Nazareth as the promised Messiah, the study of the New Testament aroused new questions in his mind and it took a considerable time before they were cleared.

He felt a very strong urge to write down some of his findings in order to assist others who might be disturbed or confused over contentions made in some quarters which minimize the value of our infallible Bible.

However, time for this particular study was very limited due to his manifold activities as a missionary and pastor of the First Hebrew Christian Church in Odessa, Russia. This Church was acknowledged by the Russian Government under the name "Church of Jewish Evangelists" because the State Church refused to apply the name "Christian" to Jews who became believers in Christ Jesus as the Saviour and Lord outside of the official Church which claimed to have the monopoly on calling herself "Christian."

Now the Lord has found the right time for the writer to prepare manuscripts on this subject for publication. In his eighty-fifth year and the sixty-second year of his Gospel-ministry, the Lord laid him aside, on a bed of sickness away from the office where so many duties demanded his full attention daily. He could now dedicate his entire time to this vital subject, and with the help of his secretary, Miss Voelker, who untiringly took dictations, and of the typists, in the office, especially Mr. Cockburn the publication of this manuscript has been made possible.

ii

If this volume shall have such an acceptance as did the one which the author published in the German language under the title "Das Wesen der Erlosung", "The Essence of Redemption"°, he will feel well rewarded and deeply grateful to the Lord for the prolonged time of his illness.

The friends who listened to the presentation over the radio of some portions of this book and ordered a complete copy of the same when it should come off the press will understand the reason for the delay. It is being published with a prayer to the Lord that He will bless this effort and use it to His glory.

VARIOUS MANIFESTATIONS OF THE DEITY, AS WE FIND RECORDED IN THE BIBLE

INTRODUCTION

The discussion presented in this volume is based entirely upon the Holy Scriptures, the Word of God, the Bible.

When we use the term "Bible" we mean the entire Book, consisting of the Old Testament and the New Testament. These, in fact, are one.

That which we call the "Old Testament" is called in Hebrew "The Tenach" (T.N.K.) which is divided into three sections. The "T" stands for *"Torah,"* the Mosaic Law which we find in the Pentateuch, the first five books of the Bible." The "N" stands for *"Neviim"*, the Prophets, the "K" stands for *"Katuvim"* the so-called "Hagiographa", that division of the Old Testament which is not included in the Law and in the Prophets.

The New Testament also consists of three sections, the *Gospels* (four in number), the *Epistles* (or letters of the Apostles) the Book of *Acts* and the prophetic Book, the *Book of Revelation.*

All of these Books deal with the Manifestation of the Diety.

Those who do not acknowledge the Holy Scripture in its entirety—no matter how much of the same they may believe to have been divinely inspired—cannot have a correct conception about the Eternal One or of His various Manifestations. They are estranged from God, no matter *who* they may be or *what* they call themselves, whether they are people of the *Old Covenant* or people of the *New Covenant.*

It is well-known that many things about the Eternal were concealed in the Old Testament and are *only revealed in the pages of the New Testament,* of which one of the most important is the "mystery of godliness" that God manifested Himself "in the flesh".

We read in the First Epistle of Paul to Timothy, *"Without controversy, great is The Mystery of Godliness; God was manifested in the flesh, justified in the Spirit, seen of angels, preached unto the Gentiles, believed on in the world, received up into glory."* (*I Tim. 3:16*)

The Sages of old who did not acknowledge Jesus Christ as the promised Messiah nevertheless believed in *three* distinctive appearances of God, namely, as "the Father", as the "Shekinah Glory", which was visible to the High Priest when he entered into the Holy of Holies in the Sanctuary over the Ark of the Covenant between the two Golden Cherubim, as well as to the people, above the Tabernacle or the "Mishkan," in the Cloud ascending from the Holy of Holies, and as the Holy Spirit, or the "Ruach Hakodesh."

They believed in those three revealments of the Diety as *being united in One.*

Such is the case even today, and it is clearly so expressed in the Liturgic worship of the Jewish people, in their communal services in the synagogues or privately at home, not only at the time of the High Festivals but in private daily worship. A brief prayer is repeated by every man when he puts on his philacteries and his prayer shawl (talles) in the name of "the *Unity,* the Holy One, blessed be His name, the Shekinah and the Hidden One."

In this little introductory prayer the Jews pronounce their belief in God, the Holy One, in the visible Shekinah, and in the hidden Holy Spirit, which they consider as a "unity," as "ONE", not realizing that it is a "Triunity". Were they to realize what they are saying, they would not consider it strange when they learn that Christians believe in God, as the *Father,* in the Messiah, as the *Son,* and in the Holy Spirit, Whom they worship as a *Triunity* as well.

Without the various Manifestations of the Eternal, of Whom the Bible speaks in the Old Testament and in the New Testament, God would remain an everlasting "Mystery," hidden and far away.

To this effect the author of the present discussion can bear his own personal testimony, how *unsatisfied* he was with all of his religious conceptions, even as a rabbinical student, until *"the mystery of godliness"* was revealed to him in the pages of the New Testament. From his early childhood until his eighteenth year, he approached God with a certain "formula" of worship and prayer set forth by the Rabbis, which gradually caused much confusion in his mind. That prayer is called "Yigdal" and we quote a few excerpts from it:

"Magnified and praised be the living God: He is and there is no limit in time unto His being.

He hath neither bodily form nor substance; we can compare naught unto Him in His holiness.

He was before anything that hath been created, even the first; but His existence had no beginning.

Behold, He is the Lord of the universe; to every creature He teacheth His greatness and His sovereignty.

The rich gift of His prophecy He gave unto the men of His choice, in whom He gloried.

There has never yet arisen in Israel a prophet like unto Moses, one who hath beheld His similitude.

The Law of truth God gave unto His people, by the hand of His prophet, who was faithful to His house.

God will not alter or change His law to everlasting for any other.

He watcheth and knoweth our secret thoughts; He beholdeth the end of a thing before it existeth.

He bestoweth lovingkindness upon a man according to his work; He giveth to the wicked evil, according to his wickedness.

He will send our Anointed at the end of day, to redeem them that wait for the end, His salvation.

In the abundance of His lovingkindness God

will quicken the dead. Blessed forevermore be His glorious name!"

In that same Prayer-Book for recitation by the Congregation we find the following lines:

"He is our God; He is our Father; He is our King: He is our Saviour; and He will save us and redeem us a second time: and He in His mercy will let us hear a second time, in the presence of all living. Behold, I have redeemed ye in the latter end, as I have done at first, to be to you for a God. I am the Lord your God."

In these prayers the Jew admits that it is unthinkable to consider God as an absolute "Yachid," namely, as a solitary One but also as an "Echod" which implies Unity. If the Jew would consider earnestly *what* he says in this daily prayer, he would surely have no reason for arguing about these two different words.

The difference is made only because of the pagan polytheists, who believed in many self-made idols and worshipped the same, whereas Jehovah declared Himself to be the One true and living God, the One, alone, whom Israel should worship as their God.

This is clearly expressed in Jehovah's own declaration from Mt. Sinai:

"I (Jehovah) *am the Lord thy God, which brought thee out of the land of Egypt, from the house of bondage. Thou shalt have none other gods before Me." (Ex. 20:1–3).*

In that same declaration from Mt. Sinai, Jehovah declared that *He* was the One who created *"heaven and earth, the sea and all that in them is." (Ex. 20:11)*

It was also emphasized by Moses, when he gave to the children of Israel the "Shma Israel", *"Hear ye, nation of Israel, Jehovah, our God is ONE."* This statement concerning Jehovah wherein the term "Echod" is used, cannot be interpreted otherwise than *ONE.*

It is also strongly emphasized by the apostle Paul in the course of his Epistle to the Ephesians where we find the following expressions:

"There is ONE body, and ONE Spirit, even as ye are called in ONE hope of your calling; ONE Lord, ONE faith, ONE baptism, ONE God and Father of all, Who is above all, and through all, and in you all." (Eph. 4:4–6)

The word used in the Hebrew rendering of this

passage is "Echod" which strongly emphasizes its meaning.

This, however, does not contradict the teaching of the same apostle concerning the *Triunity of the Diety.*

It should not be overlooked in this connection that in the record of creation found in the Book of Genesis, the Creator is spoken of as "Elohim", which is a plural form. The question as to what kind of plurality it represents will be dealt with fully in another section of this discussion.

We fully realize the serious nature of this study, and it is our deep desire to share with lovers of the Bible some of our findings in the divine "Treasury" of the Holy Scriptures.

DEITY MANIFESTED
IN CREATION

This is an entirely Scriptural subject, found in both sections of what we call "the Bible", namely, the Old Testament and the New Testament.

For many years I searched for light to enable me to answer the numerous questions which reached my desk, asked by Christians as well as Jews. It was not easy to find the right replies to satisfy the people in those two groups.

To rabbinical *Jews,* God is "hidden" in the secrecy of *Eternity* surrounded by angels and arch-angels, which are His "ministering spirits." The Jews, being "estranged" from the New Testament, do not accept it as authoritative: yet only the New Testament (or New Covenant) reveals God, Who in the Old Testament was largely concealed.

However, there are various Manifestations of the Deity in the Old and the New Testament which must be made clear to both groups.

The Old Testament sometimes "lifts the curtain" and gives us a glimpse into Eternity.

1

The first verse of the first chapter of the Book of Genesis is rendered in most of the translations as:

"In the beginning God created the heaven and the earth."

This is a record of the first creation, as well as the first Manifestation of the Diety.

The Hebrew text is somewhat different from the translations. The word "Bereshith" translated "in the beginning" literally means *"at first"*. This becomes clear when we look into other Scriptures where the same word is used, like "the first fruit," "the first sheaf," "the first born son."

The second word in the Hebrew text of Gen. 1:1 is "Barah" which means "created". The third word is "Elohim" meaning "God," while the fourth and fifth words indicate that which He created "at first" namely, the "Shamaim and the Eretz" (the heaven and the earth).

In some quarters there is speculation as to the term "Elohim" which has been translated "God" (singular) though in Hebrew it is a *plural term*, seeking to bring into the opening verse of the *Old Testament* that which is described only in the pages of *New Testament* namely, "the Holy Trinity". Although

2

in the Old Testament we have God described as "the Father", the "Shekina Glory" as the visible "appearance" of God, and the Holy Spirit "hovering over the waters", to the Jew these are just three different descriptions of God.

The term "Elohim" is unquestionably the plural of *El*, or *Eloh*, which is descriptive of God as the Omnipotent, the Almighty in Whom all powers are united. Other Scriptures prove helpful in understanding this term, which we find, for instance, in the description of the *mighty men of Moab*, mentioned in the "Song of Moses" *(Ex. 15:15)*, where they are called "*Eli*-Moab", or where mighty trees, like the Cedars of Lebanon are mentioned for which the Hebrew word is "Arze-*El*"; for lofty hills the word is "Hari-*El*", etc.

The term "Elohim", as one Who had "much power" or "more power than others," was applied to *people* as well. We read in chapter 7 of the Book of Exodus that when God delegated His servant Moses to appear before Pharaoh, the ruler of Egypt, and demand that he should let the people of Israel go free, he made Moses "an Elohim" (rendered "a god" in our English version), meaning that He made

3

him "stronger, more mighty, than Pharaoh and his magicians." Likewise "judges" in Israel were called "Elohim" because of the authority or power which they possessed to render judicial decision in difficult cases.

Speaking of contentions or "speculations", we know that such have been made in regard to the record of creation contained in the first chapter of the Book of Genesis, to the effect that "the earth was *made void* and uninhabited by a cataclysm caused by Satan, so that this record is not that of the *first* creation but of a *second* creation.

That is a very ominous contention, because the references made in support of it are in the 14th and 45th chapters of the prophecy of Isaiah, which cannot be applied to the "earth" referred to in Genesis 1, but must be applied to the *Land of Israel,* which was "made void" by Nebuchadnezzar, the arrogant King of Babylon, when he invaded the Holy Land. This can clearly be seen from the context in the two chapters above mentioned. The Land of Israel was reinhabited when the people returned from captivity in Babylon. The term "Eretz" means "soil", "ground", "land", as well as "earth".

4

We learn from Scripture that there was a time when all the people on earth spoke but *one language* with a very limited vocabulary which was the reason why one word has several different meanings, made clear only by the context.

The record of Genesis 1 enumerated six days of Creation, on the first of which *the Light* was called into existance, *God's first creative act.*

"And God (**Elohim**) *said, LET THERE BE LIGHT, and there was light.*

And God saw the light that it was good: and God divided the light from the darkness.

And God called the light Day, and the darkness he called Night. And the evening and the morning were the first day."

We find in this first chapter of Genesis the description of all that has been created on the consecutive days of which the climax was the creation of Man.

The question might be asked, "Why did the Creator plan to create the visible universe called 'the Shamaim and the Eretz' and particularly human beings — knowing, as the Omniscient One, what would take place because of the subtle temptation

5

of Satan, the archenemy of mankind?'' It was because the Eternal knew that the Manifestation of Himself by creating the universe would be more appreciated by humans, than by celestial beings. Moreover human beings would have greater need of Him, of His various attributes or characteristics than celestial beings would have.

In the creation of Adam, the first man, there was something very special.

"God (Elohim) *said, Let us make man in our image, after our likeness."* (Gen. 1:26)

Notice the plural terms "us" and "our" in this passage of Scripture. However, in the very next verse the singular term is used, for we read:

"So God (Elohim) *created man in His own image, in the image of God created He him, male and female created He them."* (Gen. 1:27)

The plural terms "us" and "our" and the singular terms "His" and "Him" are used interchangeably. We should not forget that in "Elohim", translated as "God" we have two parts: "Eloh" (singular) and the suffix "im" which makes it *plural*.

There is something else which needs to be emphasized, namely, that the creation of Adam was a *dual one,* an "Ish" (masculine) and an "Isha" (feminine). In other words, in the body of Adam, the "Ish" (man) there was included the "Isha" (woman). They were not created as two separate beings but *as one.*

Again we quote:

"So God (Elohim) *created man in His own image, male and female created He them." (Gen. 1:27)*

By a specific creative act, the "Isha" (woman) was taken out of the body of Adam, the "Ish" as we find recorded in the chapter immediately following:

"But for Adam there was not found a help meet for him. And the Lord God caused a deep sleep to fall upon Adam, and he slept, and He took one of his ribs, and closed up the flesh instead thereof.

And of the rib which the Lord God had taken from man, made He a woman, and brought her unto the man. And Adam said, This is now bone of my bones, and flesh of my flesh: she shall be called Woman, because she was taken out of man." (Gen. 2:20—23)

Before the "Isha" was removed from the body of Adam, God breathed into him His own breath:

7

"The Lord God formed man of the dust of the ground, and breathed into his nostrils the BREATH OF LIFE, and MAN BECAME A LIVING SOUL." (Gen. 2:7)

The Hebrew terms rendered as *"a living soul"* are "Nishmat hayim". Thus both Adam, "the Ish", and "the Isha" became "living souls" equally equipped and endowed in a manner entirely different from all the other creatures, which were only created as "living beings" (Nephesh hayah"). The second chapter of the Book of Genesis contains a very important record of the creation of Man in addition to the record in chapter 1, where the creation of the physical universe is described as accomplished in six days.

The second chapter tells us what took place on "the seventh day" before the Creator "rested from all His work which He had made." (Gen. 2:1, 2)

If you will read carefully, in sequence, chapter 1, chapter 2 and chapter 3 of the Book of Genesis, the full picture will develop before your eyes.

The universe, the Cosmos, was created by the Word of the Creator.

In Hebrew it is "Davar", in the first translation

into Aramaic, (a Hebrew dialect) it is "Mimrei", in the Septuagint, the Greek translation of the Old Testament made at Alexandria for Greek speaking Jews, it is "Logos", later in the Latin version it is "Verbum". This is corroborated in the New Testament, in the first chapter of the Gospel according to John, which declares that all was created, "in the first place," by the *Word of the Almighty Creator;* and in that same chapter we read:

"THE WORD WAS MADE FLESH, and dwelt among us and we beheld His glory, the glory as of the only begotten of the Father full of grace and truth." (John 1:1)

The events which are recorded in the second and third chapters of the Book of Genesis are very significant. Chapter 2 commences as follows:

Thus the heavens and the earth were finished, and all the host of them.

AND ON THE SEVENTH DAY God ended His work which He had made." (Gen. 2:1, 2)

One of those events is that which took place in the life of Adam. The other things mentioned in these chapters are the planting of the Garden (the Garden of Eden, as we speak of it), the tempting of the

"Isha" by Satan, the arch enemy of mankind, and the tragic consequences of Adam and Eve yielding to that temptation, thereby bringing upon themselves and their posterity a great tragedy, something which should never be overlooked. Adam and the "Isha" were driven out from the Garden, from the presence of God, in fact, and their fellowship with Him was severed.

It was outside the Garden of Eden that Adam called the "Isha" "Chava", rendered in our English Bible as "Eve", meaning "Mother of all living," and she bore him two sons, Cain and Abel.

It was in the Garden of Eden that God first promised the *coming of the Saviour of Mankind,* as well as the doom of Satan. *(Gen. 3:15)*

When Eve bore her first son, she believed that *he* was the one whom God had promised, and she called him "Cain", saying,

"I have gotten (Hebr. "Kanite"—purchased) a MAN from the Lord."

When she bore her second son, she being disillusioned, called him "Havel" (Abel), which means "Vanity", as all her hopes and expectations had come to naught.

10

Adam and his posterity became subjected to Satan and were under his influence. We find many vivid descriptions in the Bible of the condition of humanity. The Prophet Isaiah declares:

"We are all as an unclean thing, and all our righteousnesses are as filthy rags (or as a filthy garment) and we all do fade as a leaf, and our INIQUITIES, like the wind, have taken us away." (Isaiah 64:6)

We have the words of King Solomon to this same effect:

"Who can say, I have made my heart clean, I am pure from my sin? (Prov. 20:9)

David, the King, confessed:

"Behold, I was shapen in iniquity, and in sin did my mother conceive me." (Ps. 51:5)

Mankind needed to be *redeemed* and to have fellowship with God restored. Satan used every means at his disposal to hinder the realization of this aim, and to thwart *God's Plan of Salvation.*

When the miraculous Incarnation took place, by which Jesus Christ, the second "Adam" came into the world to be the Redeemer, Satan wanted to cause Him also (like the first Adam) to disobey God, so

11

that He, too, would fall under His (Satan's) influence, but Satan failed in all of that. Jesus did not yield to any of Satan's temptations. "Christ Jesus was obedient unto death, even the death of the Cross" and thus became the *Saviour of mankind. (Phil. 2:8)*

Hence, every human being who believes in Christ, yields to Him and acknowledges Him as Saviour, is redeemed from the power of Satan and saved for all eternity. God's decree to that effect is:

For God so loved the world, that He gave His only begotten Son, that whosoever believeth in Him should not perish, but HAVE EVERLASTING LIFE." *(John 3:16)*

12

GOD'S MANIFESTATIONS
TO THE PATRIARCHS

NOAH

The apostasy among the people increased more and more. In the time of Noah, *he* was the only one, according to the Biblical record, who did not relinquish faith in the Almighty. He was an upright man in that apostate, paganized, wicked generation. The people resisted the working of the Holy Spirit, and willfully rebelled against God, so He decided to wipe out that sinful generation by means of a great *Flood* or *Deluge*. However, in His mercy God revealed to Noah what would occur and told him to prepare a boat, a waterproof *Ark,* for the preservation of himself and his family.

This boat or *Ark* was not designed to serve humanity at large, though some people seem to think that whoever wanted to save his life could enter into the Ark for safety.

The Ark was divided into three sections or "stories". One section was for Noah and his family, (his wife and three sons with their wives): another section was for some specimens of every living creature (see *Gen. 6 & 7*) and a third section for the needed provisions. The Ark had only one door, which the Lord shut after Noah and his relatives had entered. And then the flood came. The great Deluge broke out upon the earth and this is how the Bible describes what caused it:

"The fountains of the great deep were broken up, and the windows of the sky were opened. And the rain was upon the earth forty days and forty nights."

After the Flood had subsided, Noah and his family emerged safely. A new human generation was started by Noah's three sons, Shem, Ham and Japheth. We shall not dwell upon this as the story is so well-known to readers of the Scriptures.

ABRAHAM

To begin to carry out His *Plan of Salvation for Mankind,* God needed a man, whom He could trust, a man whose faith could be tested and would come out

14

of the testing as pure gold, a genuine unfaltering faith. Such a man God found in the person of Abram, whose name was later changed to Abraham.

In His Omniscience God foresaw that Abraham's life and walk will become an example for all future generations through which mankind will learn to know the difference between *mere belief* in the existence of a Supreme Being Whom they might call Deity or God and *actual faith* and *trust* in Him despite all trials and testings of life.

Abram was seventy-five years of age when God called him out of his country, from his kindred and from his father's house to go into an unknown land. And *"Abram believed God"*, the Bible says, and obeyed His bidding. What a radical change! His ancestor's on his father's side were Amorites, on the mother's side—Hittites according to the Biblical record, which means that they and—consequently—Abram himself were idol-worshippers *(Deut. 26:5; Ezek. 16:3)*. Now this remarkable change in his belief has taken place!

God has manifested Himself to him as the Most High, the El-Elyon, possessor of heaven and earth and Abram believed *Him,* not only *in* Him. This new

15

belief, this new faith in the Most High gave him courage enough to step out into the open and confess it to people wherever he went on his journey to the land towards which God was leading him.

When God revealed Himself to Abram He promised that Abram would become the father of a Great Nation destined to be a blessing to all "the families of the earth" (the Hebrew word used to describe this nation is "Goi-Echod"), but God also promised that Abram will be the progenitor of many nations (Goim), as well.

Bidding Abram to step outside of his tent and pointing to the starry skies above his head God said unto him "so shall thy seed be". And "Abram believed in the Lord and He counted it to him for righteousness". *(Gen. 15:5, 6)*

Now the time came when God could start testing Abram's belief and teaching him the great lesson of seeing the difference between real *faith* and mere belief; that *faith* in the One true, living, eternal, Almighty God, the Elohim, Who alone is worthy to be worshipped and trusted is required, and not mere belief that He is higher and mightier than all so-called gods.

Although Abram and his wife Sarai were now well advanced in age and Sarai had given up hope of becoming a mother, God reiterated His promise that they would have a son, but they still had to *wait* for the fulfillment of it. Sarai was the one who really suffered most because of their childlessness. She had failed to give her husband a son and heir, and in those days for a married woman to remain barren was considered a disgrace or a sign that she was in disfavor with God. Sarai was experiencing dark days of depression and in her despair suggested a compromise in order to give Abram a child which she could legally claim as her own, according to the custom of those days, so Sarai gave her Egyptian maid Hagar to Abram to be his wife.

Abram yielded to her suggestion having lost hope in a miracle that would enable Sarai herself to become a mother. Thus Ishmael was born. This was a side-stepping on the part of Abram, a faltering of his faith and it ended in complete failure.

The Almighty now appeared to Abram as the *El Shaddai, God of All Sufficiency,* to make of him a father of many nations emphasizing that this covenant was to be an everlasting one. At that time his

17

name Abram was changed to Abraham.

With this renewed promise, God revealed to Abraham that his son "after the flesh" would not be counted as his seed, but only his "son of promise", born of his wife Sarah.

Both were now much older, and the Biblical record is that Abraham laughed heartily at such a possibility. *(Gen. 17:17)* But the testing of his faith continued until Abraham reached his 99th year and Sarah her 90th year. Altogether from the time of the first promise about twenty-five years had passed.

A special promise was made to Sarai, whose name too, was changed to Sarah, when three celestial messengers appeared, and promised that she would have a son. But she too, laughed at this promise and received a rebuke because of it. She was informed that in a year's time she would become the mother of a son whom she was to call Isaac, meaning "Laughter", as a reminder of her lack of *faith* in the divine promise.

The promise was fulfilled, Isaac was born.

At this same time God covenanted with Abraham and commanded that every male in his household should be circumcised. In this Covenant of Circumcision Abraham's son Ishmael was included as well as all the slaves in Abraham's household. Ishmael was then thirteen years old and Abraham was ninety-nine years of age. *(Gen. 17:23, 27)*

In the days of the prophets the necessity for circumcision was strongly emphasized, as this constituted a mark of distinction or difference between the people of Israel and the surrounding Gentile nations; but stressed even more strongly was the need to be "circumcised in heart". The prophet Jeremiah declared:

"Behold the days will come, saith the Lord that I will punish all them which are circumcised with the uncircumcised; Egypt, and Judah, and Edom, and the children of Ammon, and Moab, and all that are in the utmost corners, that dwell in the wilderness: for all these nations are uncircumcised, and all the house of Israel are uncircumcised in the heart." (Jeremiah 9:25, 26)

The Lord Jesus spoke of "circumcision of the heart" as the *New Birth*, through the operation of the Holy Spirit, as we find recorded in *John 3:1, 8)*. We are told of Nicodemus, a Rabbi in high standing,

19

an Elder of Israel, a member of the High Court, who came to Jesus to enquire how he could become an heir to the heavenly kingdom. The Lord Jesus informed him that "unless a man is born of the (Holy) Spirit he cannot enter into the kingdom of God."

At the time when God revealed to Abram, that he was chosen to become the father of a great and numerous nation and that the Land into which He brought him out of Ur of the Chaldees shall be their inheritance, He also revealed to him what would take place in the life of his posterity, his seed, in some distant future before they will enter into that inheritance. This was done in a very mysterious and awesome way which made a deep impression upon Abraham.(It is described in *Gen. 15:9, 17*) Abraham's posterity was to suffer affliction in a strange land for the period of 400 years, and be in slavery there. After the 400 years had passed God would severely punish their oppressors; and Abraham's seed would be permitted to come out of it with great wealth and take possession of the land of their inheritance. *(Gen. 15:13, 14)*

God also revealed to Abraham that the period of testing of his posterity, who were later known as

20

"the children of Israel" would be such a lengthy one not as a punishment, but for the sake of the pagan nations which at that time were occupying the Land promised to Abraham and his posterity because the measure of God's longsuffering towards them would extend to 400 years. Those nations would thus have sufficient time, either to repent of their iniquity or else "to fill up the measure of their iniquity" so that it would be justifiable to take the Land from them.

While Isaac was a source of delight to his parents and they had reason to laugh joyously when calling him by his name, Ishmael, who also lived in their household was a source of deep aggravation and dismay to Sarah, because he mocked and ridiculed Isaac to the extent that there was no other way out of the dilemma than to send Hagar and her son away. Abraham was encouraged by the Lord to do this. *(Gen. 21:9, 21)*

It is quite important to notice what the New Testament states concerning Hagar and Ishmael and about Sarah and Isaac: in Galatians 4:21, 31 the great difference between that which is of the flesh and that which is of the Spirit is clearly

21

pointed out.

God's Plan and His decision concerning Ishmael and Isaac as to the heritage was that Ishmael and his posterity, the Arab Nations, could not be considered as heirs to "the promised Land" or as having any share therein. This is a very important point, especially in view of the present conflict between the posterity of Ishmael (Arabs) and the seed of Abraham (Israel). That conflict should not be considered from the standpoint of sympathy or politics, but as being a matter of God's explicit *will*. If the "Will" of a *man* usually cannot be contested or set aside, how much more is that the case with the Will of *the Almighty!*

The time arrived when according to God's plan Abraham's faith had to undergo its severest testing. The Lord appeared unto Abraham and commanded that he should take his son, his dearly beloved Isaac, his only begotten one in accordance with the divine promise, and offer him up as a sacrifice, a burnt offering, on one of the hills of Moriah. (*Gen. 22*)

On the following morning, without any questioning or hesitancy, Abraham arose early and took his beloved son Isaac with him, and also two servants,

22

after preparing the wood and the fire which would be required for a burnt offering on the altar. They started out on the long journey, and apparently father and son remained silent most of the way. When they were approaching their destination, Isaac said to his father, "Behold the fire and the wood, but where is the lamb to be sacrificed?" His father responded, "My son, God will provide Himself a lamb." *(Gen. 22:108)*

Upon reaching the appointed hill at Moriah, Abraham, in obedience to God's command, prepared everything for the sacrifice, and bound his son, who was silent and submissive, to the altar. The father held the knife in his hand and was about to slay his beloved son, when suddenly there was a voice from heaven saying: "Abraham, Abraham lay not thine hand upon the lad, neither do thou anything to him, for now I know that thou fearest God seeing that thou hast not withheld thy son, thine only son from me. *(Gen. 22:11, 12)*

Then Abraham beheld a ram which had become entangled in a thicket by its horns, and sacrificed it instead of his son.

It is in commemoration of this event that the

23

Jews use a Ram's Horn as the "Shofar" which they blow on New Year's day, called in Hebrew "Rosh Hoshannah" pleading with God to remember the merits of Abraham and Isaac in connection with that solemn event on Mount Moriah.

What took place there is the clearest foreshadowing type of that which occurred on Calvary many years later, when the Lord Jesus stood on one of the hills, in that same vicinity, called "Golgotha," and there, as the Lamb of God was sacrificed; but it is well to note that He voluntarily laid down His life and shed His blood for the remission of the sin of the world. *(John 1:29)*

Incidentally, it is also well to note that the spot dedicated by King David for the building of the Temple, and purchased by him from Araunah the Jebusite, was likewise located in the land of Moriah. *(II Sam. 24:18 ff)*

ISAAC

Isaac grew up to manhood and was the joy and pride of his parents. The experience on Mount Moriah did not pass without leaving a deep impression upon Isaac's character. Following in the footsteps of his father, he had a deep faith in God and was a man of prayer. We find him "meditating in the field at eventide," praying, entreating the Lord.

In Gen. 25:10 we read that after the death of Abraham God blessed his son Isaac and in Gen. 26:24, the record is that the Lord *appeared* unto him and said,

"I am the God of Abraham thy father: fear not, for I am with thee, and will bless thee, and multiply thy seed for my servant Abraham's sake."

The Lord confirmed to Isaac the promise given to Abraham:

"I will perform the oath which I sware unto Abraham thy father. And I will make thy seed to multiply as the stars in heaven, and will give unto thy seed all these countries; and in thy seed shall all the nations be blessed. Because that Abraham obeyed my voice, and kept my charge, my commandments, my statutes, and my laws." (Gen. 26:3c,5)

The marriage of Isaac and Rebekah is one of the loveliest episodes in Scripture with a great spiritual significance. Isaac and his wife Rebekah

25

had experiences similar to those of Abraham and Sarah. They too, were childless for a number of years. Rebekah was greatly concerned about her barrenness, and shared her sorrow with her husband. Being a man of prayer, Isaac took the matter unto God in fervent supplication until the answer came.

When Rebekah became aware that she was about to become the mother of twins, her concern was: "which of the twins will be considered as the first-born." God revealed to her that the first to be born would *not* be the divinely chosen one, but that it will be the *younger* of them. At the time of Rebekah's delivery the first of the twins came out covered with reddish hair, so they called him Esau, which means "hairy", the second infant followed holding the heel of his brother. What name was he to bear to give significance to that most unusual occurrence? It was decided that the best name would be "Jacob", which means "Heelholder". Everything went on peacefully in the family.

"And the boys grew: and Esau was a cunning hunter, a man of the field, and Jacob was a plain man; dwelling in tents."

In this passage we find the Biblical description

26

of the characters of both sons of Isaac and Rebekah and it is well to note that the word used in the Hebrew language, which is translated "a plain man" referring to Jacob is "Ish tam", which means "blameless" or "perfect". It is the same word which we find in Gen. 17:1 in connection with Abraham, when God admonished him to walk before Him and be perfect.

Jacob spent most of his time at home and was in close relationship with his mother, while Esau, as a hunter, a man of the field, won his father's heart providing savory venison for his meals.

At the time when the aged Isaac felt that the day of his departure was approaching a dramatic event took place in the life of his family.

All her life Rebekah kept in her heart what God revealed to her before her sons were born, namely, that the younger would be entitled to receive the blessing of the first-born. So when she learned that Isaac desired to bless his sons before he died she became very anxious to see Jacob really receive it.

Esau did not care for his birthright anyhow, he "despised" it, as the Scriptures call it, which is evident from the fact that one day when he returned

27

from a hunting trip, tired and hungry, *he sold* it to Jacob for a pottage of lentils to which Jacob volunteered to add his bread.

Esau transferred his birthright to Jacob by an oath. Thus it became a legal transaction according to the customs of those days.

On the day when Isaac was ready to bless his sons Rebekah took matters in her own hands and by disguising Jacob secured the blessing of the first-born for him. (See *Gen. 27*)

The whole matter can be viewed from three angles:

1. **From the viewpoint of Esau** who forgetting the legal transaction between him and his brother became outraged to the point of wanting to kill Jacob and called him "Schemer" and "Supplanter" as if that was the right interpretation of the name "Jacob".

2. **From the viewpoint of Mother Rebekah**, who acted according to her inner conviction based upon the revelation she received.

3. **From the viewpoint of God** Who, after all, has chosen Jacob and identified Himself with him as the "God of Jacob" and as

28

previously God revealed himself to Abraham and to Isaac, He revealed himself to Jacob as well.

JACOB

On his flight from Esau, away from home, at night, in the desert, where he lay down to rest, with his head upon a stone for a pillow Jacob experienced God's presence in a very remarkable dream of great significance . . . God manifested Himself to Jacob in this vision in the same way as He did to Abraham and Isaac and confirmed His promise about their posterity and the Land they were to possess. (See *Gen. 28:11, 15*)

"And Jacob awaked out of his sleep, and he said, Surely the Lord is in this place, and I knew it not. And he was afraid, and said, How dreadful (or awesome) is this place! This is none other but the house of God, and this is the gate of heaven. And he called the name of that place "Beth-El" (the house of God). (Gen. 28:16, 19)

Jacob remained in favor with God and received

29

many blessings from Him. The greatest experience in the life of Jacob was God's manifestation to him in that lonely place where

"a man wrestled with him until the breaking of the day" (Gen. 32:24)

God dealt with him there

"face to face" therefore Jacob called the place *"Peniel,"* meaning *"the face of God."*

At this time God gave Jacob a new name — "Israel", which is interpreted

"Prince of God" or *"Mighty Victor".*

The new name, Israel, was given to Jacob not because the Lord disliked his old name. Many times in the Scriptures we find him called Jacob and the Lord being identified as "the God of Abraham, Isaac and Jacob." —

It is well to recall at this point that God predicted to Abraham that his seed would become "strangers in a strange land". Now the time came for the fulfillment of this prediction and it started with the migration of Jacob and his family to Egypt.

At that time Jacob's long missed son Joseph, who was sold by his brethern into slavery, was found occupying the position of what we would call today,

30

viceroy of Egypt, because with divinely endowed wisdom he saved Egypt and the surrounding countries from starvation at the time of severe famine.

The grateful Pharaoh advised Joseph to bring his father and his entire kindred to Egypt. Jacob accepted the friendly invitation and they settled in the fertile province of Goshen which was most suitable for their occupation as herdsmen of sheep and cattle.

Jacob spent the last seventeen years of his life in Egypt during which period his posterity greatly increased.

Two things of great significance must be mentioned in connection with the last days of Jacob's life.

When Joseph brought his two sons, Ephraim and Manasseh, to be blessed by Jacob, Joseph, realizing that his father's eyesight was now dimmed, placed his two sons before his father, Manasseh, as the elder, towards Jacob's right hand and Ephraim towards his left hand. But the Biblical record is that Jacob crossed his arms and placed his right hand upon the head of Ephraim and his left hand on the head of Manasseh. *(Gen. 48:14)* The fact of Jacob crossing his arms to bless the younger in preference to the elder reminds us that Jacob himself, though the younger son was considered by God as the elder also proves that on his death-bed Jacob was endowed with the gift of prophecy.

When blessing his own sons he received a divine revelation concerning Judah and became the first Messianic prophet when he said:

"The scepter shall not depart from JUDAH, nor the law-giver from between his feet, until SHILOH (The King Messiah) shall come; and to HIM, NATIONS (Hebrew "Amim"—plural) shall gather" (Gen. 49:10)

It is well to note that in the Hebrew text it is not *people* as in our English Bible but peoples or nations.

Although Jacob described his days as short and not very pleasant, nevertheless when facing eternity he evaluated them differently, remembering how the Lord had been with him and blessed him. He says:

". . . God before whom my fathers Abraham and Isaac did walk, the God which fed me all my life long unto this day . . . redeemed me from all evil." (Gen. 48:15, 16)

32

Jacob's last desire was that he should not be buried in Egypt but be returned to the Land of Canaan and interred in the place where Abraham and Sarah, Isaac and Rebecca and his own wife, Leah were buried. His wish was carried out by Joseph and the Bible tells us:

"And Joseph went up to bury his father: and with him went up all the servants of Pharaoh, the elders of his house, and all the elders of the land of Egypt. And all the house of Joseph, and his brethren, and his father's house." (Gen. 50:7, 8)

Nothing indicated at that time that not only the solemn prediction given to Abraham about his posterity, that they will be "strangers in a strange land", was being fulfilled, but that the second part of it was about to come to pass as well, namely, that they will suffer affliction there for a period of 400 years until — let us remember this — the iniquity of the people occupying the promised land will be full, thus proving God's longsuffering, but also His justice towards them.

As the years and even centuries went by the merits of Joseph were forgotten and the increasing number of the children of Israel was considered a great menace to Egypt by the Pharaoh ruling at the end of the 400 year period.

Not knowing anything about Joseph he started taking drastic measures to reduce the multiplication of the people of Israel, first by inflicting hard labor upon them and when this did not help a decree was issued that the midwives should kill every newborn male offspring in each Hebrew family. Later the parents themselves were charged to cast their male infants into the river, to drown them.

This was the climax of the afflictions which Abraham's posterity was to endure. The time for the deliverance of the children of Israel from their bondage was at hand.

GOD'S MANIFESTATIONS
TO MOSES

The man whom God had chosen to deliver Israel from bondage and to whom He manifested Himself in a special way was Moses. His story is a most fascinating one, and reveals God's marvelous provision for Israel and His wonderful dealings with that nation in her infancy.

Among the Jewish families in the land of Egypt there was a man of the tribe of Levi by the name of Amram, whose wife was named Jochebed. They had two children, a son Aaron and a daughter Miriam.

Because *"the children of Israel were fruitful and increased abundantly and multiplied, and waxed exceedingly mighty, and the land was filled with them,"* Pharaoh took drastic measures towards their annihilation. All newborn male offspring of the Israelites were to be thrown into the river.

At this crucial time Jochebed gave birth to a son, evidently without the help of a midwife. The mother "saw that he was a goodly child" and hid him for three months. When she could no longer do it, she prepared a little basket or "ark" of bullrushes, made it waterproof, put her little son into it and set it in the flags by the river's brink. The baby's sister Miriam stood at a distance to see what would happen to her brother.

"And the daughter of Pharaoh came down to wash herself at the river; and her maidens walked along by the river's side and when she saw the ark among the flags, she sent her maid to fetch it." (Ex. 2:5)

Immediately Miriam approached the Princess and inquired if she might call a nurse to care for the child. To this the Princess consented, and Miriam naturally called the child's mother to render this service.

The Princess agreed that the nurse should take the infant to her own home for a few years, until it was weaned, and then bring him back to her.

During that period Jochebed undoubtedly instructed her child that he belonged to the enslaved *children of Israel,* which he should never forget. The Princess adopted him and called him "Moses", which means "drawn from the water."

This child God had chosen to become the deliverer

36

of Israel from bondage.

Moses spent forty years in the palace of the Princess where he was instructed in all the wisdom of the Egyptians and enjoyed all the pleasures of the royal court.

"And it came to pass in those days, when Moses was grown, that he went out unto his brethren, and looked on their burdens: and he spied an Egyptian smiting an Hebrew, one of his brethren...and he slew the Egyptian, and hid him in the sand." (Ex. 2:11, 12b)

This is the Biblical record of what took place when Moses realized the condition in which his brethren found themselves.

When on another occasion Moses tried to interfere when two Hebrews "strove together", he found out that his killing of the Egyptian was known, as one of the fighting men said to him: "Who made thee a prince and a judge over us? Wilt thou kill me also as thou didst kill the Egyptian?"

When the news reached the palace, Pharaoh wanted to kill Moses, and Moses fled to the desert of Midian. There a Midianite Priest named Jethro hired him to tend his sheep. Eventually he married one of Jethro's seven daughters, Zipporah. When she bore him the first son, he called him "Gershon," which means "a stranger in a strange land". Moses remained a stranger during the 40 years he spent in the desert of Midian. His heart was with his people. He did not forget what his mother told him in his early childhood.

One day while tending Jethro's flocks at Mt. Horeb, Moses beheld a most phenomenal sight. The Bible describes it in a wonderful way:

"And the angel of the Lord appeared unto him in a flame of fire out of the midst of a bush: and he looked, and, behold, the bush burned with fire, and the bush was not consumed.

And Moses said, I will now turn aside, and see this great sight, why the bush is not burnt ... and God called unto him out of the midst of the bush and said, Moses, Moses. And he said, Here am I. And he said, Draw not nigh hither, put off thy shoes from thy feet, for the place whereon thou standest is holy ground. Moreover he said, I am the God of thy father, the God of Abraham, the God of Isaac and the God of Jacob. And Moses hid his face: for he was afraid to look upon God.

38

And the Lord said, I have surely seen the af-
fliction of my people which are in Egypt, and have
heard their cry by reason of their taskmasters; for I
know their sorrows; And I am come down to deliver
them out of the hand of the Egyptians..." (Ex.3:2,8a)

This was God's first manifestation unto Moses as "the Eternal One." It is well to note that God called the oppressed Hebrews "My people" and revealed Himself to Moses for the specific purpose that he might become their deliverer from the bondage in Egypt.

When Moses heard that he had been appointed to be God's emissary not only to the children of Israel but also to the tyrannical ruler, Pharaoh, he pleaded with the Lord to send someone else, because he felt inadequate for the fulfillment of such a task. It is no wonder that Moses felt discouraged. It is obvious that one who had spent so many years in the land of Egypt, exclusively among pagans, had only a very vague knowledge of the God of his fathers which was the case not only with Moses, but with the entire nation as well. Moses needed to know more about the God Who had appeared to him in such a remarkable manifestation. Therefore

"Moses said unto God, Behold when I come unto the children of Israel and shall say unto them, the God of your fathers hath sent me unto you; and they shall say to me, What is His name? what shall I say unto them:

And God said unto Moses, I AM THAT I AM: and he said thus shalt thou say unto the children of Israel, I AM hath sent me unto you." (Ex. 3:13, 14)

To be prepared for his solemn task Moses had to know more not only about God, but about himself and his own nature as well. The Lord showed him this in a unique manner, by some remarkable object lessons.

"And the Lord said unto him, What is that in thine hand? And he said, A rod. And he said, Cast it on the ground. And he cast it on the ground, and it became a serpent; and Moses fled from before it. And the Lord said unto Moses, Put forth thine hand, and take it by the tail. And he put forth his hand and caught it, and it became a rod in his hand."
(Ex. 4:2, 4)

What a shock it must have been to Moses to realize that his staff, the thing upon which he had been leaning, which had been his weapon, proved to be a serpent, the symbol of the origin of sin.

The second lesson which Moses had to learn was that *sin* is deeply embedded in the human heart, like leprosy which has its origin in the blood. The Lord commanded Moses to "put his hand into his bosom" When he took it out, it was "leprous as snow." Upon God's repeated command he put his hand into his bosom again, and when he took it out he discovered that God was able to *heal* and to *cleanse.* (See *Ex. 4:6, 7)* This was the third and most important lesson he learned.

These experiences changed Moses life. The once self confident man, who in his own strength undertook the hazardous step of helping his people by killing an Egyptian, became a humble man, convinced that he had no strength, and no ability whatsoever to carry out so great a mission *(Ex. 4:10).* He solemnly solicited that God would send someone else *(Ex. 4:13).* However, God not only encouraged Moses but endowed him with ability to perform outstanding miracles.

The people of Israel who had lived for such a lengthy period among pagans and had observed many astonishing things the priests of the Egyptian

41

deities and Pharaoh's magicians could do, needed to see "signs and wonders" performed by Moses which exceeded anything done by them, in order to recognize in him the leader sent from God. Therefore God endowed Moses with *power* which is described as that of "the very mighty one", by a word which was applied to deity of any kind. God said to Moses:

"Behold I make of thee an ELOHIM to Pharaoh." This word "elohim" is translated as "god".

It is well to recall that in the Scriptures the word "elohim" is also applied to judges because of the power or authority delegated to them by the Law. (See *Ex. 22:7, 9)*

As the Egyptians had many deities or "gods" with a specific name for each of them, the people wished to know more about the God Who had identified Himself as "the God of the Hebrews" and what His *name was.* So Moses asked God what he should say to the children of Israel wanting to know the name of the God whose messenger he was.

Then God manifested Himself unto Moses by His name JEHOVAH, a name which was never before known to Abraham, to Isaac nor to Jacob. In most of the translations of the Bible the name Jehovah is rendered as "the *LORD*". It is always used in the *singular form* and was never adopted by any pagan nation. The Biblical record of this manifestation is found in Exodus 6: 2, 4:

"God spake unto Moses, and said unto him, I am JEHOVAH, the LORD. And I appeared unto Abraham, unto Isaac, and unto Jacob as the EL SHADDAI; but by my name JEHOVAH was I not known to them.

And I have also established my covenant with them, to give them the Land of Canaan, the land of their pilgrimage, wherein they were strangers."

In the prophecy of Isaiah we find a similar statement:

"I am JEHOVAH (The Lord); that is MY NAME; and my glory will I not give to another, neither my praise to graven images (idols). (Isaiah 42:8)

That name, Jehovah, was a line of division between Israel and the *pagan nations* by which they were surrounded. To the name Jehovah was ascribed all the divine attributes.

The people of Israel believed Moses' message when he came to them in the name of Jehovah (the Lord); but Pharaoh mocked and said, "who is Jehovah

43

that I should harken to him and obey him?'' *(Ex. 5:2)*
He refused to let the children of Israel go free.

Authorized and empowered by God to act as an
"elohim" Moses demonstrated before the eyes of
Pharaoh miracles and signs which were to serve as
his credentials as ambassador of Jehovah, demand-
ing of Pharaoh to let the people of Israel go. Pharaoh's
magicians were able to imitate some of these signs
and Pharaoh hardened his heart and would not give
in.

Moses continued to inflict plague after plague
upon the Land of Egypt until Pharaoh's resistance
began to break down. At one point it seemed that
his stubbornness was broken, he expressed his
willingness to let the people go to worship their
God, but only for a few days, leaving their cattle
behind. Moses insisted that they were to take their
cattle along and go to a certain place where they
would receive instruction how to worship and serve
the Lord because they did not know how.

Again Pharaoh hardened his heart until the last
and most terrible plague was brought upon Egypt,
and only after that did Pharaoh yield to Jehovah's
demand to let the people leave.

This plague—the death of all firstborn in Egypt—
not only caused Pharaoh to consent to Moses' demand,
but to call for Moses and Aaron in the night to command them: "get you forth from among my people"
and urge them to leave immediately, taking with them
their herds and all that they possessed. Besides
that the Egyptians gave them all they requested
"jewels of silver and jewels of gold and raiment."
Thus the promise given to Abraham about his posterity—that they will come out from the land of their
bondage with great substance was also fulfilled.

But the most important and remarkable thing
that happened on that eventful night when the death-
angel carried out the divine judgment upon Egypt
was that he passed over the homes of the children
of Israel because they were protected in a very
special and significant way. God commanded them
to sprinkle the two door-posts and the lintel with
the blood of a lamb which had to be slain, saying:

*"When I see the blood, I will pass over you,
and the plague shall not be upon you to destroy
you, when I smite the land of Egypt." (Ex. 12:13b)*

This is commemorated by the Israelites through
all generations until this very day as the feast of

the Passover.

What a prototype this lamb, by whose blood the firstborn of Israel were saved from destruction, is of the Lamb of God Who shed His blood on the Cross of Calvary. But it was only "a shadow of things to come". The blood of the Lamb of God was shed not only to protect the children of Israel from death but to save from perishing every one who will believe in Him, Who voluntarily shed His blood for the remission of the sins of all mankind.

The children of Israel triumphantly marched out of Egypt towards the place shown to Moses, led by the Lord Himself. Great and unusual things awaited them ahead, a time of real testing.

They were marching toward the wilderness and the Red Sea, when they became aware that the Egyptians were pursuing them. They found themselves in a hopeless situation, between the hordes of Pharaoh and the waters of the sea. In a desperate situation like this Moses cried to the Lord,

"And the Lord said unto Moses, Wherefore criest thou unto me, speak unto the children of Israel that they go forward: But lift thou up thy rod, and stretch out thy hand over the sea, and divide it: and the

46

children of Israel shall go on dry ground through the
midst of the sea." (Exodus 14:15, 16)

The Hebrew expression "Horem Sesmatha"used
in this verse, can be translated in two ways—either
as "lift thy rod" or "lay aside thy rod" and stretch
out thy hand. If to accept the latter translation it
could mean that the people should not ascribe any
magical power to the rod itself, just the hand of
Moses was to show the direction. However, we
should not speculate on this, if the Bible does not
clearly reveal what the word "Horem" here used
actually means.

Moses obeyed the divine command.

"And Moses stretched out his hand over the
sea; and the Lord caused the sea to go back by a
strong east wind all that night, and made the sea
dry land, and the waters were divided. And the
children of Israel went into the midst of the sea,
upon dry ground: and the waters were a wall unto
them on their right hand, and on their left. (Exodus
14:21, 22)

The Egyptians followed, and when they reached
the middle of the sea the water engulfed them and
they were drowned. But the people of Israel reached

47

the other side safely.

"Thus the Lord saved Israel that day out of the hand of the Egyptians; and Israel saw the Egyptians dead upon the seashore. And Israel saw that great work which the Lord did upon the Egyptians; and the people feared the Lord, and believed the Lord, and his servant Moses." (Exodus 14:30, 31)

Stepping on the shore they raised their voices in a song of praise which is called in Scripture the "Song of Moses." This song will resound in Heaven together with "the Song of the Lamb", as we read in the Book of Revelation (Chapter 15:2, 4).

Then their march into the desert began.

The Exodus from Egypt was a triumph, but it took a lengthy journey before the children of Israel could enter into the promised land, Canaan.

Jehovah's objective in the deliverance of the children of Israel was not only to free them from slavery, but that they should be His people and become a channel of blessing to the Nations of the world as He promised their fathers Abraham, Isaac and Jacob.

As they went on step by step through the wilderness the lack of water and the lack of food caused murmuring on their part time and time again. Many a precious lesson they learned when God undertook miraculously and supplied their needs.

The first lesson they learned when they reached the waters of Marah, meaning "bitter". They suffered thirst for three days before they came to this oasis, and then "could not drink of the water because it was "bitter". Moses cried unto God and was shown a way to sweeten the water; thus Moses himself as well as the entire nation learned to know that He, the Lord, is the Only One to be trusted and obeyed. He manifested Himself there as *the Lord, their Healer.*

Another great lesson they learned when the Lord day after day supplied them with food, mysterious food which they called "Manna", meaning "What is it?" It was "bread from heaven" and Moses and Aaron pointed them to the fact that by this the Lord "Who brought them out of Egypt and heard their murmurings, was manifesting to them *His Glory.*

Twice during the journey through the wilderness God used Moses to give the thirsty people water from a rock. The first time the Lord said to Moses:

49

"Behold, I will stand before thee there upon the rock in Horeb; and thou shalt SMITE the rock, and there shall come water out of it, that the people may drink." (Exodus 17:6)

There was a great manifestation of the Almighty pointing to Christ the "Rock of Ages," Who was smitten (crucified) in order that the living water of Salvation may freely flow to satisfy every thirsty soul.

The second time God's strict command to Moses was:

"Take the rod, and gather thou the assembly together, thou, and Aaron thy brother and SPEAK YE unto the rock, before their eyes; and it shall bring forth his water and thou shalt bring forth to them water out of the rock: so thou shalt give the congregation and their beasts drink." (Numbers 20:8)

"Speak ye to the Rock", the Rock could not be smitten *twice*. As we said before, according to the Scripture this Rock symbolized Christ Who was "ONCE offered to bear the sins of many." (Hebr. 9:28a).

Moses, however did smite the Rock , even twice. It was an act of disobedience and could not

50

be left unpunished. God manifested His absolute justice before the eyes of the people not showing any respect of persons. Moses had to die in the wilderness, this side of the Jordan, and not lead the children of Israel into the promised land.

"And the Lord spake unto Moses and Aaron, Because ye believed me not, to sanctify me in the eyes of the children of Israel, therefore ye shall not bring this congregation into the Land which I have given them." (Numbers 20:12)

The last Manifestation of God to Moses was a very solemn one, when God declared to him that he was to die. What God revealed to Moses concerning the children of Israel at that hour was expressed by him in an awesome prediction:

"For I know that after my death ye will utterly corrupt yourselves, and turn aside from the way which I have commanded you; and evil will befall you in the latter days; because ye will do evil in the sight of the Lord, to provoke him to anger through the work of your hands." (Deut. 31:29)

Moses was also inspired by God to write and teach the children of Israel a song of praise and worship to remind them of all the marvelous works

51

of the Lord and His dealings with them from the beginning. It concludes with this serious admonition.

"Set your hearts unto all the words which I testify among you this day, which ye shall command your children to observe . . . for it is not a vain thing for you . . . it is your life." (Deut. 32:46, 47)

Before parting from his people Moses blessed each of the 12 tribes with a special benediction and brought before their mind the fact that the Lord loves the *Nations.* It is very significant that in the Hebrew original verse 3 of chapter 33 of Deuteronomy reads:

"Yea, He loved the peoples"

(Am-im, plural) and the term used for love is the strongest of all definitions of love mentioned in the Bible. (Af Chovev Amim.)

Moses, the great Leader of Israel, the Giver of the Law, which is ascribed to him, kept his title "Ish Elohim" (man-elohim) which was given to him when he was sent to Pharaoh to demand the release of the children of Israel from bondage, till his very end and his death was a triumph of faith.

He silently ascended Mount Nebo as God had commanded, ready to die. From there God showed him the entire promised land.

"And the Lord said unto him, This is the land which I sware unto Abraham, unto Isaac, and unto Jacob, saying I will give it unto thy seed. I have caused thee to see it with thine eyes, but thou shalt not go over thither.

So Moses the servant of the Lord died there in the land of Moab, according to the word of the Lord. And He buried him . . . no man knoweth of his sepulchre unto this day." (*Deut. 34:4, 6*)

The words rendered in this passage as "Moses died . . . according to the *word* of the Lord," can also be translated "Moses died . . . by the *Mouth* of the Lord". This unusual statement was interpreted by the ancient Jewish sages as "Moses died by a kiss from God."

Joshua, the son of Nun who was Moses' assistant during the years of Israel's wandering through the desert, became his successor to lead the children of Israel over the Jordan into Canaan. He was also the one who wrote the concluding part of the Book of Deuteronomy, wherein we learn of the end of Moses' life. He pays great tribute to Moses in his statement found in Deut. 34:10, 12.

"And there arose not a prophet since in Israel like unto Moses, whom the Lord knew face to face, In all the signs and wonders which the Lord sent him to do in the land of Egypt to Pharaoh, and to all his servants, and to all his land. And in all that mighty hand and in all the great terror which Moses shewed in the sight of all Israel."

Moses experienced many a wonderful manifestation of God during his lifetime. The Lord spake unto Moses "face to face as a man speaketh to his friend."

At the time when Moses needed reassurance as to his calling, when he asked the Lord to show him His way, the Lord said to him "My presence shall go with thee and I will give thee rest."

When Moses besought the Lord to show him His glory, the Lord instead—because no man can see God and live—said unto him:

"Behold, there is a place by me, and thou shalt stand upon a rock: And it shall come to pass, while my glory passeth by, that I will put thee in a clift of the rock, and will cover thee with my hand while I pass by." (Ex. 33:21, 22)

It seems the Lord wanted to unfold to Moses the

54

mystery of the Rock foreshadowing Christ. What a blessing this was to Moses when he stood upon the Rock and God's hand covered his eyes!

The greatest manifestation of God took place at Mt. Sinai at the time when the Ten Commandments were given and the Covenant between God and Israel established.

The Lord manifested Himself in an awesome way with thunders and lightnings and other great phenomena and a thick cloud upon the mountain, from which the voice of the Lord resounded in order that the people might hear it and believe Moses forever. *(Ex. 19:9, 16)* When the frightened congregation implored Moses:

"Speak thou with us and we will hear, but let not God speak with us lest we die." (Ex. 20:19)
the Lord revealed to him that a prophet greater than Moses, more worthy to be God's spokesman, will be sent to them:

"I will raise them up a Prophet from among their brethren, like unto thee, and will put my words in his mouth; and he shall speak unto them all that I shall command him." (Deut. 18:18)

This prediction cannot be applied to any of the

other prophets who came after Moses, as they all pointed to the One Who would eventually come, namely, the promised Messiah and Saviour, Jeshuah (Jesus). He alone would have authority to speak and to act in the place of Jehovah. He is the only One Who could declare, "I am the Way, the Truth, and the Life"—"The Words which I speak unto you are Spirit and Life"—"I and the Father are ONE". Jesus Christ is the incarnate Living Word, "God manifested in the flesh." *(I Tim. 3:16)*

THE MANIFESTATIONS
OF JEHOVAH TO ISRAEL

During the long period of their bondage in Egypt the children of Israel were surrounded by idol worshippers, therefore they had a very vague conception about God and did not have any knowledge of how to worship Him. While Moses was dealing with Pharaoh concerning Israel's liberation he confessed that even he, himself did not know how to serve Jehovah.

It was necessary for the people of Israel to learn to know God, as the Holy One, and receive instruction about the ways to worship Him. God revealed Himself to them as the Only One to be worshipped and served and avouched Himself to be their God.

"I am Jehovah, thy God, which have brought thee out of the land of Egypt, out of the house of bondage." (Ex. 20:1)

He was the *only One* Who freed them from their slavery, not Moses nor any other "elohim".

God also revealed to the children of Israel the purpose for which He delivered them, namely, that they should be His "peculiar people" (Am segula) His "royal priesthood" (Mamlechet kohanim), a "holy nation" (goy kodesh) to serve Him in full obedience and to keep His commandments. Nevertheless God did not impose His will upon them. They themselves expressed their willingness to obey saying:

"All that the Lord hath spoken we will do." (Ex. 19:8)

The great and majestic manifestation of God to Israel at Horeb or Mt. Sinai became the center of the Old Covenant. The account of the happenings there is filled with dramatic events. (See *Ex. 20:1—22*) The people were overwhelmed by the awesome way in which God declared to them His Law, the Decalogue, the Ten Commandments. At that time they were more than willing to fulfill what the Lord demanded from them, but very soon they experienced that mere good intentions were of no avail. This was expressed in later times by the Apostle Paul in Rom. 7:19, where he says:

"The good that I would, I do not, but the evil which I would not, that I do."

When Moses who was called by God to ascend

58

Mt. Sinai "drew near unto the thick darkness where God was" to receive the Ten Commandments inscribed on two tables of stone, tarried there, the people of Israel thinking that they had lost their leader became desperate. They gathered around Aaron complaining:

"This Moses, the man that brought us up out of the land of Egypt, we wot not what is become of him". (Ex. 32:1)

and demanded that he make them an "elohim" to lead them on.

From the account which Aaron gave to Moses about this fateful event we receive an idea as to how it came about. First of all, it can be seen that the people were quite aggressive in their demand that Aaron should make them "gods" (Hebrew "elohim"). He said, to Moses: "Thou knowest the people that they are set on mischief", which according to the Hebrew text means "they are in the grip of the wicked one". Aaron may have thought it would not be so easy for them to part with their gold or perhaps he hoped that Moses would return before any action was taken by him, but he was pressed by the people to act quickly. Note the words: *"Up,* make gods who shall go before us!" They needed something visible, like the gods of the Egyptians. They did not ask Aaron to make them a Jehovah, nor raise up for them another leader like Moses, they wanted an "elohim". Pressed hard by the people Aaron cast all the gold they brought to him into the fire and the molten metal took on the shape of a calf.

The people immediately gathered around this idol and started to worship it, declaring it to be the god, who brought them out of Egypt.

Moses descended from the mountain carrying the two tablets on which God Himself had inscribed the Ten Commandments and when he saw the calf and all that went on there ne became very angry and "cast the tables out of his hands and brake them beneath the mount." (*Ex. 32:19 f.*) He also destroyed the golden image, and ordered that all who had not taken part in this terrible sin but were still loyal to the Living and True God Jehovah, should gather around him. Those who so assembled themselves were of the tribe of Levi, and Moses commanded that they should execute divine justice upon those who had been guilty of worshipping the golden calf. Three thousand of the disloyal people fell. (See

Ex. 32:25—28)

Moses was heart-broken. He separated himself from the apostate people and went to a distant place, pitched the "Tabernacle of the Congregation" there and remained in seclusion until he received another revelation of God. Those who were willing to separate themselves from the rest "who sought the Lord" came to him, as a testimony of their faith and loyalty to God, Jehovah.

If the people of Israel had considered what took place on Sinai when they refused to listen to the Voice of God at the tenth Commandment (so that He ceased to speak to them) they would not dare call Sinai "the summit of summits" as they do. The corrupted human nature needs more than just Commandments. The nations of the world could not be satisfied with *only* Ten Commandments. This is the reason why the Law of Moses did not have the same effect among the Nations as the Gospel message proclaimed by the promised Messiah, Jesus, the Message of *the Salvation,* which He accomplished on the summit called Mt. Calvary.

This tragic portion of Israel's history in their relationship to Jehovah is very significant: God's

61

righteous judgment was ready to descend upon the guilty nation, His decree was their utter destruction, but Moses interceded in a most marvelous way for his apostate brethren to the point that he prayed to be blotted out from God's Book of Life, if He were not willing to forgive the grave sin of his people. He reminded the Lord of His promises to their fathers Abraham, Isaac and Jacob and pleaded with Him to guard the honor of His Name among the surrounding nations who would look with contempt upon such a severe judgment over a nation which He Himself so gloriously delivered from their bondage in Egypt. This prayer of intercession found favor in the eyes of God — it reminds us of the passage in Ezek. 22:30 where we read that in a similar situation the Lord "sought for a man that should stand in the gap before Him for the land, that He should not destroy it, but found none". Here Moses did this very thing and the Lord revoked His sentence and confirmed His promise to be the God of Israel.

"And he said, Behold I make a covenant: before all thy people I will do marvels, such as have not been done in all the earth, nor in any nation . . . (Exodus 34:10a)

62

Again Moses was called by God to ascend Mt. Sinai, where he was to receive a copy of the Decalogue inscribed on two tables of Stone similar to the first ones, but it is well to note and very significant that on these tables was a change made in the Commandment concerning the Sabbath Day. This Commandment in the first version reads:

"Remember the Sabbath day to keep it holy . . . for in six days the Lord made heaven and earth, the sea and all that in them is, and rested the seventh day: wherefor the Lord blessed the Sabbath day, and hallowed it". (Ex. 20:9 and 11)

In the second it sounds differently.

There *another reason* is given for keeping the Sabbath:

"Keep the Sabbath day to sanctify it, as the Lord thy God hath commanded thee. Six days thou shalt labour, and do all thy work: but the seventh day is the Sabbath of the Lord thy God . . . and remember that thou wast a servant in the land of Egypt and that the Lord thy God brought thee out thence through a mighty hand and by a stretched out arm: therefore the Lord thy God commanded thee to keep the Sabbath day." (Deut. 5:12—15)

In the first version of this Commandment God

the Creator proclaimed His desire that the people of Israel should share in the joy of His own spiritual rest, which He entered with delight and satisfaction upon finishing the work of Creation, that by sacred resting they could participate spiritually in the accomplishments of their Creator.

After the people of Israel turned away from Jehovah and instead of worshipping Him made themselves an image, a golden calf and considered it their god, it is obvious that they could no longer share the spiritual rest of the Creator.

But God did not withdraw Himself from the children of Israel, after they had broken the covenant which He made with them; He showed His unchanging love by calling Himself in the new version of the Ten Commandments, *their God as well*. Only their rest on the Sabbath day became a physical, rather than a spiritual one in the deeper sense of the word as it was intended to be in the beginning. It became a memorial day for them to remind them they had been slaves in Egypt, actual slaves, (not in a spiritual sense) and had been delivered by the Lord of this slavery. Therefore this seventh day of rest cannot be made applicable to any other nation, than the nation of Israel, it belongs to them exclusively. It is also important to keep in mind that no commandment concerning the Sabbath day was ever given to any man, not even to Abraham, Isaac or Jacob, but only to the children of Israel after their deliverance from bondage.

Under the New Covenant we do not find any "seventh day rest" commanded to the Church. The believers in the Lord Jesus Christ on their own accord gathered together for worship "on the first day of the week" commemorating the Lord's *resurrection* from the dead. The *spiritual* rest of the New Testament believer is that rest which he has in Christ.

All the Laws and Statutes which the Lord commanded Moses to give to the people of Israel are contained in the Book of the Law, the "Toreth Moshe", highly revered by the nation of Israel till this day.

"Moses commanded us a law, even the inheritance of the Congregation of Jacob."
These were the "oracles of God" entrusted to them and preserved by them for all future generations.

However, the Law was not a means of justification in the sight of God, nor was it a means of Salvation. It was given to unveil or reveal the *sin* deeply

65

rooted in the human heart and the need of salvation and redemption from sin. It was our schoolmaster to bring us unto Christ that we might be justified by faith.

No New Covenant believer, no Christian, should ever put himself under obligation to keep the Law or try to observe that which was commanded exclusively to the children of Israel under the Old Covenant.

There is no other Gospel than the one proclaimed by Christ and His disciples; there is no other Name whereby we can be saved *(Acts 4:12)* than the Name of Jesus which means Saviour.

To ignore this name is a grave and ominous error widely spread in our days.

The Lord Jesus after His resurrection enjoined His disciples to be His witnesses. Witnesses of His miraculous incarnation, of His vicarious death by crucifixion and of His victorious resurrection from the dead. No true Christian should ever bear any other name than that of a Witness of Jesus Christ.

God's manifestations to Israel, His wondrous dealings with that nation are kept and preserved on the pages of the Holy Scriptures as examples for admonition and a warning for those who live in the last days. *(I Cor. 10:11)*

GOD'S MANIFESTATIONS
IN THE SANCTUARY

At the time when Moses ascended the "holy mountain" where he received the Ten Commandments, he was also given detailed instructions how to build a Sanctuary, a place of worship for the children of Israel, a place where God Himself could dwell among them.

Moses was given a pattern of the Tabernacle, or "Mishkan," where God's holiness was to be revealed by means of visible objects conveying a deep spiritual meaning and significance which were also to be foreshadowing types and symbols of the promised Messiah. As we read in Hebrews 8:5 they were "to serve as an example and shadow of heavenly things."

This Tabernacle was to be built by means of free-will gifts of the people. Every gift no matter how small was accepted, no one was excluded from the joy of giving and the people brought in so much of everything necessary for the outfitting of the Sanctuary that Moses had to ask them to cease bringing their contributions.

The order of worship was also explained to Moses — the various sacrifices to be brought and their meaning and purpose — all pointing to the One Who was to come to be the perfect sacrifice once and forever.

The Tabernacle was divided into three sections: one for the assembling of the people; one for the priests in which to officiate; one exclusively for the High Priest where he would enter only once a year. This was called the Holy of Holies.

The Holy Place of the Sanctuary where the priests performed their special services contained the Seven-branched Candlestick, the Golden Altar of Incense, the Table of Shewbread with its twelve loaves called the "lechem ha panim," which were sanctified for the use of the priests and renewed daily.

Each of these objects pointed to Christ, the Messiah, the Light of the World, the Bread of Life, as well as to many others of His attributes and denoted the purpose of His coming.

The main part of the Tabernacle was the Holy of Holies, in the center of which was the Ark of the Covenant or Ark of Testimony. It was covered by a

"Kaporeth", called in our English Bible "the Mercy Seat," upon which were the two Golden Cherubim. The Ark contained several significant objects — all of them witnesses *against* the people of Israel, reminding them of their sins and failures. They were put there at the explicit command of Jehovah and were *covered by the Mercy Seat.* These were: two stone tablets called "Tables of Witnessing" (Hebrew: Lichot h'eduth); reminding the people of the ones which Moses destroyed in his righteous indignation when he saw the people worshipping the golden calf. Then a golden vessel containing an omer of manna was to be kept in the Ark for reminding future generations of the murmuring of the children of Israel about the food miraculously provided for them by the Lord in the barren wilderness.

The third significant object placed in the Ark was the rod of Aaron, which budded, bloomed and brought forth fruit when Korah and his followers rebelled against him. Thus the Lord confirmed Aaron's priesthood, the divine assignment to serve in the Tabernacle of the congregation for Him and his sons. Later to the contents of the Ark was added the book of the law, the book in which Moses had written, as commanded by God, all that happened to the children of Israel during their journey through the wilderness, "that it may be there for a witness against them" (*Deut. 31:26*)

The Sanctuary was built for the special purpose which is expressed in God's order to Moses: "Speak unto the children of Israel . . . and let them make me a sanctuary that I may *dwell* among them" (*Ex. 25:8*)

In that Sanctuary the presence of the Lord was manifested in a way visible to the whole Congregation of Israel as the Shekinah, a cloud which ascended from the Mercy Seat, from between the two golden cherubim and rested on the "Mishkan", the Tabernacle (the Hebrew word Mishkan is derived from the same root "Shekan" as the word Shekinah — meaning "to dwell"). During their long journey through the wilderness God was always with them visibly as the Shekinah, going before them as a Cloud during the day and as a Pillar of fire in the night. This was a special token of God's grace and mercy to the people He had chosen, reassuring them of His constant presence, saying as it were,

"Lo, I am with thee!"

70

The Tabernacle was to be the only place where the children of Israel were to commune with their God and this by ways and means He provided for that purpose.

As we mentioned before, the Law of Moses was a "Schoolmaster" to bring the people to the realization not only of their sinfulness but also of their weakness and helplessness. It was to reveal their sinful condition, to awaken in their innermost being the desire for atonement, forgiveness, redemption, the longing for the coming of the promised Messiah, the Saviour, the Deliverer . . .

Until His coming, until the Day of Redemption, God's grace and mercy provided a means of temporary atonement for sins and transgressions, namely, the various sacrifices offered by the sanctified priesthood—first in the Tabernacle, later in the Temple.

These sacrifices had an entirely different meaning than the sacrifices and offerings brought by the surrounding heathen nations to their gods or idols which were to reconcile, to appease them.

The sacrifices ordered by God were not to be *gifts to Him on the part of the people.* Many times Moses, Isaiah and other prophets rebuked the people

71

for their misconception of the meaning and purpose of the same.

We read in Isaiah 1:11

"To what purpose is the multitude of your sacrifices unto me? saith the Lord: I am full of the burnt offerings of rams and the fat of fed beasts; and I delight not in the blood of bullocks or of lambs, or of he—goats."

David fully understood that when he said:

"Thou desirest not sacrifice, else would I give it; thou delightest not in burnt offering." (Ps. 51:16)

In the Book of Leviticus detailed instructions are given as to the various types and kinds of sacrifices for different kinds of sins and transgressions, but all of them bear the name "Korban" (derived from the root "Korov", meaning "to draw nigh", to approach). All these represented a means provided by God for the people's approach to Himself. Leviticus 17:11 distinctly points out that all sacrifices offered in the sanctuary were God's gift to the sinful nation:

". . . The life of the flesh is in the blood: and I have given it to you upon the altar to make an atonement for your souls; for it is the blood that

72

maketh atonement for the soul."

It was God Himself who made it possible for the people to use the blood of an innocent clean animal as a substitute to cover their iniquities. The animal was to die in the sinner's stead, to satisfy divine righteousness and justice which decreed:

"the soul that sinneth should die."

All the instructions concerning sacrifices do not constitute a *demand* on God's part to bring Him sacrifices. They were only intended to teach the people how to use *His* means of atonement in the right place and in the right manner. It was not to be done arbitrarily and not as an immitation of the practices carried out by the heathen.

THE DAY OF ATONEMENT

The services, rituals and sacrifices prescribed for the Day of Atonement are of special significance and demand full attention and consideration, being of such great importance in the relationship between Jehovah and His people under the Old Covenant and presenting the greatest of all foreshadowing types and symbols of Christ and His sacrificial vicarious death.

The Day of Atonement was to be observed with great solemnity and its main objective was the offering of three distinct Sacrifices, consisting of a bullock, a ram and a goat (one of the two brought before the Lord). Only on that day the high priest, who officiated, was allowed to enter into the Holy of Holies behind the veil. After Nadab and Abihu, the two sons of the high priest Aaron had to die because they brought "strange fire" before the Lord *(Lev. 10:1, 2)*. God commanded that the high priest was not to come at *all times* into the holy place within the veil before the mercy seat . . . that he die not" *(Lev. 16:2)*. Being a sinful man himself, Aaron (or any other high priest) could not serve as mediator between the people and their God before his own sins were *covered* by the blood of a substitutional sacrifice.

The sacrifices offered in the Sanctuary, especially on "Yom Kippur" the Day of Atonement, were—as before stated—God's provision for the *covering* of sins (this is the meaning of the word Kippur, derived from "Kapar"—to cover).

Thus the first of the three appointed animals— the bullock—was to be offered as a sin-offering for the high priest and his house before he could act as mediator for the people.

He was to lay aside his garments of glory and beauty, put on vestments of pure white linen and carry the blood of his own sacrifice into the holy place to sprinkle it seven times on the Mercy Seat, while the Holy of Holies was filled with a cloud of sweet incense strewn over glowing coals from the altar—a symbol of ascending prayers. *(Rev. 5:8)*

Now the high priest was able to offer sacrifices for the people.

Two goats were brought to the entrance of the Tabernacle. Upon these goats the high priest had to cast lots to determine which one was to become the sin offering. The other is called the "scapegoat". There is something obscure, something mysterious about this goat and we shall deal with this subject after we say a little more about the sin—offering and the way its blood was sprinkled over the Mercy Seat, which is of great significance, as well.

In the same manner as the blood of his own sin-offering was brought into the holy place by the high priest, he carried the blood of the goat appointed as sin-offering for the people behind the veil and sprinkled it over the Mercy Seat seven times in the form described in the synagogical liturgy as "Kemazlof." It was to be done as a "Zelem" later changed into "Zelef" (as the letters m and f are interchangeable in the Hebrew). The reason for this change is obvious: the word "Zelem" means "like a cross" or "like an image" (in the modern Hebrew used in the State of Israel "zelem" means photograph, picture).

However, the significance of this sevenfold sprinkling in such a form can only be explained by what we find in the Scriptures. The sin-offering was a *substitutional sacrifice* of an innocent animal dying in the sinner's stead. According to the Law of Moses every person who had to pay the death penalty; after he had been executed, usually by stoning, was to be *hanged on a tree,* not by the neck as in modern times, but with outstretched arms, thus forming the shape of a cross. *(Deuteronomy 21:22, 23)*

Therefore the blood of the substitutional sacrifice representing the death of the sinner was sprinkled upon the Mercy Seat in such manner as to demonstrate the complete picture of the execution of the sinner as prescribed by the Law, to show that all the requirements of God's justice had been met.

Again we must remind ourselves that all that was prescribed by the law was only "a shadow of good things to come" and that,

"those sacrifices which were offered year by year could never make the comers thereunto perfect."

For it is not possible that the blood of bulls and of goats should take away sins." (Hebrew 10:1 and 4)

These were only foreshadowing types of the One perfect and everlasting Sacrifice of the only begotten Son of God Whom He *gave* because He so loved the world and Who Himself voluntarily *gave* His life as a propitiation for the sins of mankind.

About the second goat brought to the door of the Tabernacle we read:

"The goat on which the lot fell to be the scapegoat shall be presented before the Lord to make an atonement with him and to let him go for a scapegoat into the wilderness". (Lev. 16:10)

There is something mysterious about this goat, as we said before, and we find that some translators do not even attempt to interpret the term used in the Hebrew text, namely, "Azazel" and instead of "let him go for a scapegoat into the wilderness" render this passage *(Lev. 16:10)* as "send it away for Azazel into the desert."

The best Bible commentators agree that this term "Azazel" means an evil spirit or demon. It consists of two parts Az and Azel, of which the first can be translated as cruel, impertinent, vehement, insolent and the second as "roaming about", truly, a fitting description of Satan. In the Holy Scriptures the wilderness is often denoted as the place of habitation of evil spirits. (See *Isa. 13:21, 22; 34:10—14*) The Lord Jesus, too, was "led into the *wilderness to be tempted of the devil*" *(Matthew 4:1)*

What had to be done with that goat which remained

78

alive is described in Lev. 16:21, 22:

"*And Aaron shall lay both his hands upon the head of the live goat, and confess over him all the iniquities of the children of Israel, and all their transgressions in all their sins, putting them upon the head of the goat, and shall send him away by the hand of a fit man into the wilderness:*

And the goat shall bear upon him all their iniquities unto a land not inhabited; and he shall let go the goat in the wilderness."

By this procedure the high priest in the name of the whole congregation of Israel declared and confessed that because of their sins and iniquities they were bondslaves of Satan, the father and originator of evil, and now were willing to separate themselves from him, returning as it were that what belonged to him: namely, their sins resting upon the head of the goat.

In the Jewish Prayer book among the prayers for the New Year and the Day of Atonement is found an interesting account about the procedure with the Scapegoat, or the goat for the Az-Azel.

After all the foregoing was completed the high priest called one of the priests to lead the goat away into the desolate wilderness and tie it by a woolen twist to a rock upon a steep hill, then push it down backwards. Before the goat could reach the foot of the hill, his limbs were shattered. The messenger who had led the goat into the desert supposedly said: "Thus may the sins of the people of the house of Israel be wiped out." This is an excerpt from a talmudic interpretation of this procedure, but, of course, we cannot go beyond that which is mentioned in Scripture concerning this mystery.

The services in Israel's sanctuary, first in the Tabernacle and later in the Temple of Jerusalem were of great significance and value as foreshadowing types and symbols of the great Salvation wrought by Jesus Christ, the promised Messiah of Israel, the Saviour of the world. They were part of the manifold and various manifestations of the true living God, part of His great Plan of Salvation conceived in Eternity and worked out in the course of human history.

GOD'S MANIFESTATIONS
TO THE PROPHETS

ELIJAH

"God . . . at sundry times and in divers manners spake in times past unto the fathers by the prophets" *(Heb. 1:1)*. These words of Scripture plainly state the role which the true prophets played in human history. God spoke through them, He declared His will "by the mouth of His holy prophets" *(Luke 1:70)*. He revealed the future to them and they wrote down for coming generations all that the Lord wanted them to know. The Apostle Peter says in his second Epistle (1:19–21):

"We have also a more sure word of prophecy; whereunto ye do well that ye take heed as unto a light that shineth in a dark place until the day dawn, and the day star arise in your hearts: knowing this first that no prophecy of the Scripture is of any private interpretation. For the prophecy came not in old time by the will of man: but holy men of God spake as they were moved by the Holy Ghost."

The prophets were God's messengers, preachers of repentence, constantly reminding men of the great

81

things which God had done in ages past and revealing God's great Plan of Salvation.

They appeared on the scene of Israel's history in the days of gross apostasy: Israel was divided into two kingdoms. Ten tribes established not only a separate political state but also a new religious cult: they worshipped two Golden Calfs erected by their leader Jeroboam in two places of worship. Two tribes in the beginning remained faithful to God and continued to serve Him in the Temple at Jerusalem. However, after a while they too, turned away from the Lord and although they continued to worship in the Temple and observed the rituals and forms prescribed by the Law of Moses, their sinful conduct drew them farther and farther away from God.

Despite the great apostasy of the so-called Kingdom of Israel, God did not forsake them entirely and during the rule of one of the most wicked of their Kings, Ahab, sent to them His mighty witness, the prophet Elijah.

At that time Ahab's wife Jezebel who was a Phoenician, introduced to the people the cult of Baal, the main Phoenician deity.

Through the prophet Elijah God manifested His

supreme power in a great and majestic way:

The encounter of Elijah with the prophets of Baal is one of the most remarkable events of Old Testament history.

After three years of drought and famine in Samaria God sent Elijah to announce to Ahab, that He was going to send rain upon the earth. Fearlessly Elijah accused Ahab of his apostasy and ordered him to gather "all Israel and the prophets of Baal and the prophets of the groves which eat at Jesebel's table" and Ahab obeyed.

It is well to recall that all the prophets of Baal and of the groves, 850 by number, pleaded with Baal all day long in front of their sacrifice to send fire from heaven to consume it, they shouted and cried, they cut themselves with knives "until their blood gushed out upon them" with no result whatsoever.

On the other side we see the lonely figure of God's prophet calm and sure of his divine calling, challenging them to put forth more effort in their pleading, because their "mighty god" could be busy with other things and therefore unable to hear them.

At the time of the evening sacrifice when there still was "neither voice nor any to answer, nor any that regarded" Elijah said unto all the people, "Come near unto me . . . And he repaired the altar of the Lord that was broken down." A new altar was built, everything for the sacrifice was prepared and not only drenched with water, but surrounded by a trench filled with water and then Elijah raised his voice in a solemn prayer:

"Hear me, O Lord, hear me, that this people may know that thou art the Lord God, and that thou hast turned their heart back again.

Then the fire of the Lord fell, and consumed the burnt sacrifice, and the wood, and the stones, and the dust, and licked up the water that was in the trench.

And when all the people saw it, they fell on their faces: and they said, The Lord, he is the God; the Lord, he is the God." (I Kings 18:37—39)

God not only demonstrated on that day His Omnipotence and Glory but also fulfilled the promise given through Elijah, his faithful servant, and sent a great rain upon the Land.

Time and time again the Lord sent His prophets to the whole nation of Israel: Elijah, Elisha, Jonah, Amos, Hosea and others were sent especially to the ten-tribed Kingdom until the time when their apostasy brought upon them the righteous wrath of God and they were taken into captivity by the king of Assyria. According to God's decree their kingdom has never been restored.

To the Kingdom of Judah many prophets were sent, each of them with a special task and a special message, but all revealing God's great Plan of Salvation and predicting the Coming and the Work of the Messiah.

The first place among these prophets is occupied by

ISAIAH

The Lord has given to this prophet great and mighty revelations concerning the past, present and future not only of israel but the surrounding kingdoms, as well.

The ministry of Isaiah who was sent to the tribes of Judah and Benjamin starts with two remarkable *visions*.

First, he saw the condition in which the nation found itself in those days. Their sinful state could be compared only to the state of Sodom and Gomorrah and they deserved utter destruction, just as those

85

wicked cities did, but the Lord had mercy upon them and remained faithful to His promise given to their fathers (See Isaiah chapters 1—5).

The second vision we find recorded in the sixth chapter of the Book of Isaiah. The Hebrew word used here for *Vision* means rather *revelation:* he *"saw* the Lord sitting upon a throne, high and lifted up and his train filled the temple," as the Lord of Hosts surrounded by seraphim who "cried unto one another 'Kodesh, Kodesh, Kodesh!' — Holy, holy, holy is the Lord Sabaoth, the whole earth is full of His glory." *(Isaiah 6:3)*

This manifestation of the greatness and holiness of Jehovah, sitting upon His throne, of which the psalmist once said that "righteousness and judgment are its foundation" (Ps. 89:14a), not only filled the heart of the prophet with awe, but made him realize his own sinful condition. The celestial atmosphere, the very presence of God in which he found himself caused him to exclaim:

"Woe is me! for I am undone; because I am a man of unclean lips, and I dwell in the midst of a people of unclean lips; for mine eyes have seen the King, the Lord of hosts" (Isa. 6:5).

86

He became conscious of the fact that he needed cleansing, especially his lips had to be purified, if he were to pronounce God's messages to the people of Israel.

"Then" — *he testifies* — *"flew one of the seraphim unto me, having a live coal in his hand, which he had taken with the tongs from off the altar; and he laid it upon my mouth, and said, Lo, this hath touched thy lips, and thine iniquity is taken away, and thy sin purged."*

Thus he experienced the second part of what the psalmist had to say about God: Whose throne's foundation is righteousness and justice, namely, that "mercy (or lovingkindness) go before His face." *(Ps. 98:14)*

Then he heard the Lord asking: "Whom shall I send, and who will go for us?" To this Isaiah now gladly responded: *"Here I am; send me."* He was ready to be God's messenger, to proclaim His word. But before he went out to speak to the people about the great and glorious events of the future, especially concerning the Messiah and the new era which would bring Jews and Gentiles together into the heavenly family, God gave Isaiah some solemn instructions. In His wisdom God wanted to keep His full plan, a secret as it were, until the Messiah would appear and accomplish His great mission, the salvation of the whole human race, when the middle-wall of partition (the Law of Moses, the Old Covenant) will be abolished and the New Covenant established. Under the economy of the Old Covenant Israel *could not understand* God's plan of *Salvation by Grace,* which is entirely contrary to the conditions of the Law. Only under this aspect can we understand Isaiah 6:9.

"Go and tell this people, hear ye indeed, but understand not, and see ye indeed but perceive not." Isaiah 8:16.

"Bind up the testimony, seal the law among my disciples."

Isaiah 29:10, 14.

". . . the Lord hath poured out upon you the spirit of deep sleep, and hath closed your eyes: the prophets and your rulers, the seers hath he covered. And the vision of all is become unto you as the words of a book that is sealed, which men deliver to one that is learned, saying, Read this, I pray thee: and he saith, I am not learned.

Wherefore the Lord said, Forasmuch as this people draw near me with their mouth, and with their lips do honour me, but have removed their heart far from me, and their fear towards me is taught by the precept of men:

Therefore, behold, I will proceed to do a marvelous work among this people, even a marvelous work and a wonder: for the wisdom of their wise men shall perish, and the understanding of their prudent men shall be hid."

This same thought is expressed by the Apostle Paul in II Cor. 3:12-16 where he speaks about "the veil of Moses" covering the eyes and the hearts of the people, and especially in Rom. 11:25 where he says:

"For I would not, brethren, that ye should be ignorant of this mystery, lest ye should be wise in your own conceits; that blindness in part is happened to Israel, until the fullness of the Gentiles be come in."

In this connection we can only exclaim with the Apostle Paul, that truly "the ways of the Lord are past finding out!" *(Rom. 11:33)*

The greatness of the prophet Isaiah developed

more and more. Vision after vision was vouchsafed to him especially concerning the Messiah, His miraculous incarnations, His suffering and humiliation, but also His exaltation, even a vision of His millenial kingdom.

The Book of Isaiah represents in miniature, the entire Bible. Like the Book of Genesis, it begins with the "heavens and the earth" and it concludes as does the Book of Revelation with a "new heaven and a new earth." It was through this prophet, Isaiah, that God issued an appeal to every believer:

"Comfort ye, comfort ye my people, saith your God. Speak ye confortably to Jerusalem, and cry unto her that her warfare is accomplished, that her iniquity is pardoned . . . " (Isa. 40:1—2)

It is not without purpose that we emphasize this 40th chapter of the prophecy of Isaiah, with its great message of consolation and forgiveness of sins—which leads directly to the message of the New Testament.

Every Christian should also remember the admonition of the Apostle Paul which is found in Romans 11:30—32.

"For as ye in times past have not believed God,

yet have now obtained mercy through their unbelief:
Even so have these also now not believed, that
through your mercy they also may obtain mercy, for
God hath concluded them all in unbelief, that he
might have mercy upon all.''

JEREMIAH

Jeremiah was chosen by the Lord to become His messenger to Israel and the surrounding nations when he was still very young. It was during the rule of Josiah over the kingdom of Judah. The word of the Lord came to Jeremiah saying:

"I sanctified thee and I ordained thee a prophet unto the nations." (Jer. 1:5)

"Say   not, I am a child: for thou shalt go to all that I shall send thee and whatsoever I command thee thou shalt speak. (Jer. 1:7)

"God's biddings are always enablings" and before sending Jeremiah out as His spokesman, the Lord prepared him for this task in a way similar to what Isaiah had experienced. His whole being was changed, when, as he testifies:

91

". . . the Lord put forth His hand and touched my mouth, and the Lord said unto me, Behold, I have put My words into thy mouth (Jer. 1:9)

Great visions were given to this prophet, great revealments of the future, even to the last days. We will not go into detail about his predictions concerning the Babylonian captivity and its duration, Israel's dispersion and regathering, and other solemn revelations which he received, but would like to call attention to the prophecy found in the 31st chapter of the Book of Jeremiah, where we read from verses 31–35:

"Behold, the days come, saith the Lord, that I will make a new covenant with the house of Israel, and with the house of Judah: Not according to the covenant that I made with their fathers in the day that I took them by the hand to bring them out of the land of Egypt; which my covenant they brake, although I was an husband unto them, saith the Lord:

"But this shall be the covenant that I will make with the house of Israel; After those days, saith the LORD, I will put my law in their inward parts, and write it in their hearts; and will be their God, and

92

they shall be my people.

"And they shall teach no more every man his neighbour, saying, Know the LORD: for they shall all know me, from the least of them, saith the LORD: for I will forgive their iniquity, and I will remember their sin no more.

"Thus saith the LORD, which giveth the sun for a light by day, and the ordinances of the moon and for the stars for a light by night, which divideth the sea when the waves thereof roar; The LORD of hosts is his name."

The Old Covenant was established between Jehovah and Israel, His people, chosen and destined to proclaim His glory. It is likened to a marriage-contract in many passages of Scripture. This Covenant was broken by the people, the relationship between Israel and God was severed. The Old Covenant lost its validity. The nation was without any Covenant, but the Lord remained faithful to His apostate people, He promised to renew, to re-establish His fellowship with them, but it would have to be on an entirely different basis: not by making them keep the Law of Ordinances, which they proved unable to fulfill, but on the basis of Grace alone, on the basis of complete regeneration. Such Covenant could and would include the whole human race, all nations on the face of the earth.

The appeal will go forth to all mankind, as Isaiah already proclaimed:

"Look unto me and be ye saved ALL THE ENDS OF THE EARTH" *(Isaiah 45:22)*

The prophet Jeremiah foretold such a complete abolition of the Old Covenant that the Ark of the Covenant of the Lord would not even be mentioned any more "neither shall it come to mind, neither shall they remember it. *(Jer. 3:16)*

There is still another remarkable prediction found in the Book of Jeremiah about the continuing value of the Passover-celebration:

"The days come, saith the Lord that it shall no more be said, the Lord liveth, that brought up the children of Israel out of the land of Egypt".(Jer. 16:14)

A greater deliverance will take place and the Lord will cause all nations "to know His hand and His might: and they shall know that His name is THE LORD." *(Jer. 16:21)*

94

EZEKIEL

Ezekiel was another great prophet to whom God manifested Himself in an outstanding way. Ezekiel was "among the captives in the land of the Chaldeans" when the Lord revealed Himself to him in an awesome vision, which is described in detail in the first chapter of his prophetic book; in conclusion of this description Ezekiel says:

"This was the appearance of the likeness of the glory of the Lord. And when I saw it, I fell upon my face, and I heard a voice of one that spake. And he said unto me, Son of man, stand upon thy feet, and I will speak unto thee."

In order to become God's messenger to the children of Israel, to be able to say to that rebellious nation: "Thus saith the Lord", Ezekiel needed to experience a special enduement of the Holy Spirit. He testifies in chapter 2 verse 2:

" . . . the spirit entered into me."

His mission was to remind the nation in bondage of the sins and transgressions that brought them into captivity; especially the young generation which grew up in the land of Babylon far away from Jerusalem and the Sanctuary, warning them against idolatry, calling them to repentance. Moreover great promises for the future were given through Ezekiel. God showed him that He will not abandon His people, but will remain faithful to the covenant made with their fathers. In Ezek. 20:42 we read:

"And ye shall know that I am the LORD, when I shall bring you into the land of Israel, into the country for the which I lifted up mine hand to give it to your fathers."

"And ye shall know that I am the Lord, when I have wrought with you for my name's sake, not according to your corrupt doings, O ye house of Israel, saith the Lord GOD."

One of the most outstanding visions of Ezekiel is the one recorded in the 37th chapter known as the "Vision of the Valley of the dry bones." Ezekiel describes it as follows:

"The hand of the Lord was upon me and carried me out in the spirit and set me down in the midst of the valley which was full of bones and caused me to pass by them round about: and behold there were many ... and lo, they were very dry." (Ezek. 37:1,2)

A hopeless picture! Can these bones live? the

Lord asked His prophet. And he could only answer: "O, Lord God thou knowest."

Later God revealed to him that these bones represented the whole house of Israel: the Kingdom of Judah as well as the Kingdom of Israel, who were in captivity in Babylon and Assyria and suffered such severe hardships, endured such great tribulations, that they came to the point when every hope of restoration was lost:

"Son of man", God said to Ezekiel, "these bones are the whole house of Israel, behold, they say, our bones are dried and our hope is lost . . ." (Ezek. 37:11)

They felt themselves forsaken by God, not realizing that such a thing was impossible. They did not remember the marvelous dealings of God with His people in the past of which the prophet Isaiah made the remarkable statement:

"In all THEIR affliction HE was afflicted, and the angel of His presence saved them: in His love and His pity He redeemed them . . ." (Isaiah 63:9)

So here again God manifests His faithfulness, sending Ezekiel to the whole house of Israel with a message of hope and comfort:

"Therefore prophesy and say unto them, Thus saith the Lord GOD; Behold, O my people, I will open your graves, and cause you to come up out of your graves, and bring you into the land of Israel.

"And ye shall know that I am the LORD, when I have opened your graves, O my people and brought you up out of your graves.

"And shall put my spirit in you, and ye shall live, and I shall place you in your own land: then shall ye know that I the LORD have spoken it, and performed it, saith the LORD."

This prophecy was literally fulfilled in the days of Zerubbabel, Ezra and Nehemiah when many of the captives actually returned to their homeland, but it seems that the fulfillment of the greatest and most important part of it still lies in the future.

In our days we see another regathering of the Nation of Israel into the Holy Land from all the corners of the earth, where they were dispersed among the nations and endured great sufferings and hardships.

"The dry bones" are coming together, flesh and skin begin to cover them, but as Ezekiel saw in his vision, there is no breath in them yet. Only the breath of God, His Holy Spirit can bring them to life.

The time will come, when the promise will be fulfilled.

"Behold, I will cause breath to enter into you and ye shall live." (Ezek. 37:5)

"And so all Israel shall be saved as it is written, there shall come out of Zion the Deliverer and shall turn away ungodliness from Jacob." (Rom. 11: 26).

DANIEL

At an early age Daniel was taken into Babylonian captivity along with other boys "of the king's seed, and of the princes . . . in whom was no blemish, but well favoured, and skillful in all wisdom, and cunning in knowledge, and understanding science, and such as had ability in them to stand in the king's palace, and whom they might teach the learning and the tongue of the Chaldeans." *(Dan. 1:3—4)*

Of these young men Daniel and three of his friends appeared to be the most outstanding ones, because they were faithful to their God "and He gave them knowledge and skill in all learning and wisdom. And Daniel had understanding in all visions and dreams."

Daniel's life-story is most remarkable. He lived and worked during the rule of Nebuchadnezzar and Belshazzar, kings of Babylon, and Darius and Cyrus, kings of Persia who conquered not only Babylon where the two tribes were captives, but also Assyria, the land of captivity of the ten tribes. Daniel proved to have an "excellent spirit," because it was the spirit of the Lord, which had full possession of him. For that reason he emerged victoriously from all his trials and caused all the kings whom he served to recognize the supremacy and sovereignty of his God.

Daniel was a man of prayer and he also studied diligently the portions of God's Word which were available to him in those days, especially the writings of the prophet Jeremiah, to whom the Lord revealed that the Babylonian captivity would last for *seventy years*. When Daniel realized that this predicted period of time was coming to an end, he "set his face unto the Lord God to pray and supplicate with fasting and sackcloth and ashes.''

Daniel applied himself so earnestly to prayer and entreaty because he was greatly concerned about the desolation of Jerusalem and was afraid that as a result of the apostate condition of the people of Israel their captivity would not be terminated at the predicted time.

He fully acknowledged the sinful state of the people and that they deserved nothing but God's righteous indignation, His wrath, and the severe punishment which His justice inflicted upon them. He identified himself with the people confessing:

"We have sinned, and have committed iniquity, and have done wickedly, and have rebelled . . .

"Neither have we harkened unto thy servants the prophets, which spake in Thy name . . . "
Then he appealed to the forgiving Grace of the Lord, pleading with Him to act according to His great mercy:

"Now therefore, O our God, hear the prayer of thy servant, and his supplications, and cause thy face to shine upon thy sanctuary that is desolate, for the Lord's sake . . .

"O Lord, hear; O Lord, forgive, O Lord, hearken

101

and do; defer not, for thine own sake, O my God: for the City and thy people are called by thy name." *(Dan. 9)*

This prayer reminds us of the great intercessory prayer of Moses, the Servant of Jehovah.

Not only was the prayer of Daniel answered, but because he was "greatly beloved by God" a great revelation was given to him. Gabriel, the heavenly messenger appeared to him at the time of the evening oblation "to give him skill and understanding" for the things he was to show him, namely, God's program for the future of Israel and the Nations of the world; exact time-periods were set up: time was divided into seventy weeks of years during which Jerusalem was to be rebuilt, the Temple restored, and the people resettled in their homeland. A later time thereafter was appointed to "make an end of sins and to make reconciliation for iniquity and to bring in everlasting righteousness, and to seal up the vision and prophecy and to anoint the most Holy;" the Messiah was to appear and to be "cut off but not for himself;" then the sacrifice and the oblation were to be caused to cease; Jerusalem was to be invaded by a mighty prince and become desolate. *(Dan. 9:24—26)*

The Lord Jesus referred to this prophecy of Daniel when He spoke about the coming destruction of Jerusalem and the Temple and wept over them. This came to pass literally in the year 70 A.D. when the Roman hordes under the command of the Emperor Titus invaded the Holy City.

To Daniel were revealed many other great things: the coming of the antichrist, the resurrection of the dead, and the everlasting Kingdom of Christ.

HOSEA

Hosea was one of the few prophets sent to the Ten tribed kingdom, which called itself the "kingdom of Israel" and as is well known, started its existence by rebellion against the descendants of king David, after Solomon's death.

Under the leadership of Jeroboam the son of Nebat, one of Solomon's servants, a "mighty man of valor" whom the king elevated to a high position, ten tribes of Israel separated themselves from the house of David not only politically but *religiously*

103

as well. *(1 Kings 11:26 f)* They turned away from the true and living God to idolatry, first worshipping golden calves and later adopting the cult of Baal and other pagan deities.

To this apostate nation the prophet Hosea was sent with a special message from God which he was to illustrate in his own life in the most dramatic way.

As we study the Holy Scriptures, especially the writings of the prophets we find that the Lord sometimes called Himself "the Shepherd of Israel", sometimes her "Father" and in some instances her "Husband." Such is the case in the unique prophetic message entrusted to Hosea.

First of all, when "the word of the Lord came unto Hosea" he was ordered to take an adulterous woman as his wife and also to take her illegitimate children into his family. After Hosea married this woman by the name of Gomer and she bore him a son, God Himself named him "Jezreel", their second child was a daughter and again it was the Lord Who named her as well: "Lo-ruhamah" ("no pity") was she to be called; the name of their third offspring, a son, was ordered by God to be "Lo-ammi" ("not my people"). This marriage, as well as the symbolic

104

names given to the children, indicates the ultimate defeat of the apostate kingdom, similar to the defeat suffered in the Valley of Jezreel, that God would no longer have pity or mercy upon the house of Israel, that He would not consider them His people any more.

However, this was not meant to be the destruction of Israel as a nation, it applied to the willfully established ten-tribed kingdom, which was to cease to exist never to be re-established politically.

The children of Israel were to "abide many days without a king, and without a prince," and without many other things, but the Lord their God was not going to forsake them forever.

To Hosea, as to all the other prophets God manifested Himself as the faithful One and Hosea's writings are full of great promises for the future. In Hosea 2:19,20 God says to Israel:

"I will betroth thee unto me forever: Yea, I will betroth thee unto me in RIGHTEOUSNESS, and in JUDGMENT, and in LOVINGKINDNESS, and in MERCIES. I will even betroth thee unto me in faithfulness: and thou shalt know the Lord." (Hosea 2: 19, 20)

The Lord revealed to Hosea that the future would hold blessing and restoration for the whole nation. We read in Hosea 1:10.

". . . it shall come to pass, that in the place where it was said unto them, Ye are not my people, there it shall be said unto them, Ye are the sons of the living God. Then shall the children of Judah and the children of Israel be gathered together . . . " (Hosea 1:10,11)

The whole house of Israel, all the twelve tribes, will be united, as one Nation, under one Sceptre, the sceptre of the Son of David, the King Messiah.

ZECHARIAH

One of the last Old Testament prophets who lived and worked among those of the nation of Israel who had returned from captivity in Babylon was Zechariah, to whom were vouchsafed remarkable visions not only concerning the near future, but about the days when the final restoration of Israel will take place, about the time when

"the Lord their God shall save them . . . as

106

the flock of His people: for they shall be as the stones of a crown, lifted up as an ensign upon his land." (Zech. 9:16)

The land shall be purified from all idolatry, when in true repentance they shall turn to God.

"In that day there shall be a fountain opened to the house of David and to the inhabitants of Jerusalem for sin and for uncleanness." (Zech. 13:1)

The fate of Israel depends entirely upon the relationship between the people and their God, and to Zechariah as to all the other prophets the Lord manifested Himself as the faithful One, whose wrath is not forever, but whose grace is everlasting.

"Again the Word of the Lord of hosts came to me, saying . . .

"I was jealous for Zion with great jealousy, and I was jealous for her with great fury. Thus saith the Lord: I am returned unto Zion and will dwell in the midst of Jerusalem, and Jerusalem shall be called a city of truth; and the mountain of the Lord of hosts, the holy mountain." (Zech. 8:1 to 3)

God's grace and mercy towards Israel ran like a golden thread through the whole Bible. He always manifests Himself as the *unchanging God.*

107

Israel received many "pledges" from God since He established His covenant with them. In Leviticus 26:44, 45 we read:

"When they be in the land of their enemies, I WILL NOT CAST THEM AWAY . . . to destroy them utterly, and to break my Covenant with them: for I am the Lord their God.

"But I will for their sakes remember the Covenant of their ancestors, whom I have brought forth out of the land of Egypt in the sight of the heathen, that I might be their God."

This statement was confirmed by all God's prophets.

MALACHI

The name of this prophet means "My messenger" and he was the last of the prophets sent to the remnant of Israel which returned to the promised land after 70 years of captivity.

His message was a message of love. Despite all Israel's failures and shortcomings, despite the sins of their priests, which he strongly condemned the promise remains:

"I am the Lord, I change not; therefore ye sons of Jacob are not consumed." (Mal. 3:6)

In this prophecy of Malachi a great promise is given for the future when the children of Israel shall return to their God. About "those who feared the Lord and that thought upon His name" the promise is:

"And they shall be mine, saith the Lord of hosts, on that day which I create as a special treasure: and I will spare them, as a man spareth his own son that serveth him." (Lit. transl. Mal. 3:17)

These promises are inseparably connected with the coming of the Messiah:

"Unto you that fear My name shall the Sun of Righteousness arise with healing in his wings." (Mal. 4:2)

PROPHECIES CONCERNING
THE MESSIAH

The prophecies contained in the Scriptures are numerous and varied. Some of them appertain to individuals, and others to nations and lands, but for the most part they have to do with the destiny of Israel.

As we were speaking about the various manifestations of God to the true prophets we were dealing mainly with the things which He revealed to them about that nation, which God chose for Himself — not because it was better than the other nations, but because in the life of Israel God wanted to work out His plans and purposes for all mankind.

God called Israel "His firstborn son", His "creation" and to them He revealed Himself in all His sublimity and greatness when He gave them His holy commandments, which in Deut. 33:2 are called "a fiery law" and because He had singled them out" from all the families of the earth" to show forth His praise, He punished them severely time and time again for their iniquities." Nevertheless despite all the divine visitations and punishments they received the promise that they would not be annihilated or utterly destroyed, but would fulfill their destiny—to be a channel of blessing to the world.

That is the reason why the greatest and most important prophecies are those which have to do with Israel and are rooted in the Messiah of Israel, the Saviour and Redeemer of the world.

The origin of the Messianic prophecies reaches as far back as to the Garden of Eden and the first Messianic prediction is found at the very beginning of the Bible.

The primal ancestors of mankind yielded voluntarily to the temptation of "the old Serpent", the "Nahash Kadmoni", the arch-deceiver Satan, despite God's warning as to the seriousness of the consequences of such a step, the fateful results of disobedience, for time and eternity. However, just as soon as the transgression of God's command separated Adam and Eve from their Creator, God manifested Himself as their Redeemer, and we find here the first confirmation of the statement made by the apostle Paul:

"Where sin abounded, grace did much more

111

abound". (Rom. 5:20)

Right there and then the first prediction was made by God Himself about the coming of a Redeemer who would destroy the arch-deceiver, "the Serpent". It was made not as a promise to Adam and Eve, but in the form of a decree of God sealing the final doom of Satan, the originator of sin, who had caused their fall:

"The Lord God said unto the serpent . . . I will put enmity between thee and the woman, and between thy seed and her seed; it shall bruise thy head, and thou shalt bruise his heel." (Gen. 3:15)

This was to be carried out at God's appointed time, but first Adam and Eve had to learn from this decree that because of God's righteousness and justice the promised Redeemer would have to atone for their sin by offering Himself as a vicarious sacrifice. They had to see first the consequences of sin manifested in their own lives, and experience the misery and suffering which sin inflicts upon the transgressor, and even death itself, "the wages of sin." All this was to make them realize their need of redemption.

The prediction made in the Garden of Eden

became a *promise* when it was given to Abraham, the first man whom God, because of his (Abraham's) faith, loyalty and obedience, could call "His friend" and could therefore reveal to him His love for all mankind, notwithstanding their grave apostasy.

The promise given to Abraham included all nations:

"In thy seed" — God said to Abraham — *"shall all families of the earth be blessed." (Gen. 12:3)*

It is well-known from the writings of the apostle Paul that by the "seed of Abraham" — the Messiah, the Saviour, is meant. (Gal. 3:16)

The promise was reiterated to Isaac and to Jacob and gives us the first proof, that *"God so loved the world."*

Now as we go through the writings of the various prophets we find that their Messianic predictions can be divided into three cycles or categories viz.:

I. Those pertaining to the coming of the Redeemer at what is called His "first advent" as to *when, where* and *how* He would come.

II. Prophecies concerning His characteristics

or attributes and the program of His accomplishments.

III.   Prophecies concerning His millennial kingdom.

The three questions as to *how, when* and *where* the Messiah was to come are answered most accurately by such prophets as Isaiah, Micah, Daniel, Haggai and others.

In the 7th chapter of the Book of Isaiah, verse 14, we are told *how* the Redeemer would come:

"The Lord himself shall give you a sign: Behold, a virgin (Heb. "H'Almah", THE VIRGIN) shall conceive, and bear a Son, and shall call his name Immanuel (meaning "God with us").

The same thought is continued in the 9th chapter of Isaiah's prophecy, where it says:

"Unto us a child is born, unto us a Son is given; and the government shall be upon his shoulder; and his name shall be called: Wonderful Counsellor. The mighty God, The Everlasting Father, The Prince of Peace." (Hebrew: "Peleh, Yoetz, El Gibor, Avi-Ad, Sar Shalom") (Isa. 9:6)

The exact *place* where the Messiah was to come is given by the prophet Micah:

114

"Thou, Bethlehem Ephratah, though thou be little among the thousands of Judah, yet out of thee shall he come forth unto me that is to be ruler in Israel; whose goings forth have been from of old, from everlasting." (Micah 5:2)

As to the *time* when the Messiah would come, we have the most remarkable calculation found in the 9th chapter of the Book of Daniel (verses 24 and 25) revealed to him in a special vision. And the prophet Haggai predicts that the glory of the second temple will be greater than that of Solomon. God revealed it to him:

"Thus saith the Lord of Hosts; . . . I will shake all nations, and the desire of all nations shall come: and I will fill this house with glory . . . in this place will I give peace." (Haggai 2:6—9)

As we consider now the prophecies concerning the characteristics and the program of the accomplishments of the Messiah, we must refer first of all to Isaiah to whom God vouchsafed most outstanding revelations about the promised Redeemer. In the 11th chapter of his prophecy we find that He would be a descendant of Jesse (the father of David), growing as a branch out of his roots and that

115

". . . the Spirit of the Lord shall rest upon him, the spirit of WISDOM and UNDERSTANDING, the spirit of COUNSEL and MIGHT, the spirit of KNOWLEDGE and of the FEAR OF THE LORD." (Isa. 11:2)

In the 61st chapter of Isaiah's prophecies we find the full program which was set forth for the Messiah to accomplish:

"The spirit of the Lord God is upon me," — *Isaiah in his prophetic vision hears the Messiah proclaim* — *"because the Lord hath annointed me to preach good tidings unto the meek; he hath sent me to bind up the broken-hearted, to proclaim liberty to the captives, and the opening of the prison to them that are bound; to proclaim the acceptable year of the Lord, and the day of vengeance of our God; to comfort all that mourn; to appoint unto them that mourn in Zion, to give unto them beauty for ashes, the oil of joy for mourning, the garment of praise for the spirit of heaviness; that they might be called Trees of righteousness, the planting of the Lord, that he might be glorified."* (Isa. 61:1—3)

His appearing is a most joyful event and the prophet Zechariah describes it in glowing colors:

"Rejoice greatly, O daughter of Zion; shout,

116

O daughter of Jerusalem: behold, thy King cometh unto thee; he is just, and having salvation; lowly, and riding upon an ass . . . " (Zech. 9:9)

The most remarkable of all the Messianic prophecies is the one contained in the 53rd chapter of the Book of Isaiah. This chapter, as the context shows, actually begins with verse 13 of chapter 52, wherein the word "Behold" draws our attention to the main subject of this prophecy — *"the Servant of the Lord."* Who is meant by this "Servant" of whom it is said in Isaiah 52:13, that he "shall deal prudently, he shall be exalted, and extolled, and be very high?" Who else, than the Messiah?

It is a common interpretation on the part of the rabbis that these words mean that "He shall be exalted above Abraham, be extolled above Moses and be very high above the angels." No one in Israel is considered greater than Abraham, there is no greater teacher than Moses, no one is holier or more able to stand in the presence of God than the angels who do His will and are His ministering spirits, but the *Messiah,* Who surpasses them all.

What is found in the 49th chapter of Isaiah definitely confirms the thought that it is the Messiah

117

of Whom the prophet speaks. There we read:

"Now saith the Lord that formed me from the womb to be his servant, to bring Jacob again to him . . . my God shall be my strength. And he said, It is a light thing that thou shouldest be my servant to raise up the tribes of Jacob, and to restore the preserved of Israel; I will also give thee for a light to the Gentiles, that thou mayest be my salvation unto the end of the earth." (Isa. 49:5 & 6)

In the following verses of Isaiah 52 we are confronted with a mystery which even deepens when we start reading the 53rd chapter:

"As many were astonished at thee; his visage was so marred more than any man, and his form more than the sons of men — so shall he ASTONISH (lit.) many nations; kings shall shut their mouths at him; for what had not been told them shall be seen; and what they have not heard shall they consider." (Isa. 52:14 & 15)

What God revealed to Isaiah in this vision fills the prophet himself with such astonishment that he exclaims:

"Who hath believed our report? and to whom is the arm of the Lord revealed?" (Isa. 53:1)

118

The Hebrew text suggests that the word "believed" here means: "Who has considered our report to be true, or who has confirmed it?"

To be able to believe the report of the prophet Isaiah about the things which were revealed to him, which were heard by him from God Himself, help from above is needed. The expression "the arm of the Lord" sums up the greatness, the glory, the power and the beauty of the Lord and can be revealed only by God's Holy Spirit.

The message following this introduction is so paradoxical to the foregoing description of the Messiah as being "exalted, extolled and very high" — that it can well be understood that without divine enlightenment it would be impossible to comprehend and to believe it. The prophet Isaiah continues:

"For he shall grow up before him as a tender plant, and as a root out of a dry ground; he hath no form nor comeliness; and when we shall see him, there is no beauty that we should desire him. He is despised and rejected of men, a man of sorrows, and acquainted with grief: and we hid as it were our faces from him; he was despised, and we esteemed him not." (Isa. 53:2, 3)

119

In the Hebrew language the same word is used for "tender plant" as is used for a "suckling infant." So it would be correct to translate this passage as "He (the Messiah) shall grow up before him as an infant, and as a root out of a dry ground." Here we have the full picture of the coming of the Messiah and the condition in which the nation finds itself at that time.

To Isaiah was given such a complete revelation of the vicarious suffering and death of the promised Redeemer that his report reads as one of an eye-witness to what actually happened.

The heart of Isaiah's message lies in the 4th, 5th and 6th verses of chapter 53 wherein after describing the rejection of the Messiah and how the people turned their faces away from Him and did "esteem Him stricken, smitten of God and afflicted," the prophet emphatically declares:

"SURELY he hath borne OUR griefs, and carried OUR sorrows . . . he was wounded for OUR transgressions, he was bruised for OUR iniquities; the chastisement of OUR peace was upon him; and with his stripes we are healed.

"All we like sheep have gone astray; we have

turned every one to his own way: and the Lord hath laid on him the iniquity of us all.''

This is one of the most outstanding revelations of God's unspeakable love and grace, which found its literal fulfillment in the Person and Work of the Redeemer and Saviour Yeshuah Hamashiach, Jesus Christ, our Lord.

THE MYSTERY OF GODLINESS

The greatest of all manifestations of the Deity was the *Incarnation,* the virgin-birth of the promised Redeemer as the Son of God, which the apostle Paul calls "the mystery of godliness." He says:

"Without controversy great is the mystery of godliness: GOD WAS MANIFEST IN THE FLESH..." *(I Tim. 3:16)*

The miraculous *Incarnation* of the *Saviour* is the *basis of our most holy Christian faith,* of which the Lord Jesus is "the Author and Finisher" and for that reason this should be emphasized in our preaching and teaching more than is usually the case.

At the beginning of human history we find God, the Omnipotent Creator, manifesting Himself to the progenitors of mankind — who willfully severed themselves from Him by disobedience — as a Merciful Redeemer as well as a just and holy God. It was at that time, back in the Garden of Eden, that God introduced His Plan of Salvation by the first Messianic prediction, that it would be *"the seed of the woman"*

122

who would conquer the enemy Satan.

"When the fulness of the time was come, God sent forth His Son, made of A WOMAN, made under the law, to REDEEM them that were under the law, that we might receive the adoption of sons." (Gal. 4; 5)

The miraculous embodiment of the Saviour was *most essential* for the carrying out of God's eternal Plan of Salvation.

The tragic events in the Garden of Eden, the falling into sin of Adam and Eve, resulted in the fact that their posterity, the whole human race, was born in sin and needed to be redeemed from the power of Satan. This necessitated a miraculous birth, the preparation of a special body for the Saviour with a living soul and with the perfect holiness of the Spirit of God Himself.

Because according to God's Plan of Redemption, the Redeemer had to shed His own blood as a vicarious sacrifice and "pour out His soul unto death." No angel or other celestial being could carry out this plan of God. It had to be a being of *flesh and blood,* of body, soul and spirit, the "second Adam", as the Apostle Paul states:

"The first man is of the earth, earthy; the
SECOND MAN *is the* LORD FROM HEAVEN. *(1 Cor.*
15:47)

"For there is one God, and one mediator between
God and men, the Man Christ Jesus." (1 Tim. 2:5)

"For as much then as the children are partakers
of flesh and blood, he also himself likewise took
part of the same; that through death he might destroy
him, that had the power of death, that is the devil."
(Heb. 2:14)

The miracle of the Incarnation, the virgin birth,
is frequently denied in our days, and it is especially regrettable that even some who call themselves
"Christian ministers" not only do not accept this
doctrine, but are definitely opposed to it. It seems
quite inconsistent that people who believe in God
as the omnipotent Creator should limit Him in regard
to miracles. Some people wholeheartedly believe in
creation of man from the dust of the earth, as orthodox Jews do, yet reject the very thought of the incarnation of the Messiah through the Holy Spirit of
God.

In his great Messianic vision the prophet Isaiah
declared:

124

"Hear ye now, O house of David . . . the Lord Himself SHALL GIVE YOU A SIGN: Behold, a virgin (in the Hebrew original — H'Almah, THE virgin) shall conceive, and bear a Son and shall call his name "Immanuel" (meaning "God with us" Isa. 7: 13, 14).

Isaiah further describes the Child as *the Son* to Whom divine characteristics are attributed:

". . . the government shall be upon his shoulder and his name shall be called Wonderful, Councellor, The Mighty God, The Everlasting Father, The Prince of Peace." (Isa. 9:6)

How could the prophet declare such things, if not by divine inspiration and revelation? How can the virgin-birth of the Saviour be questioned when it was foretold centuries before by one of the greatest prophets of the Old Testament and came to exact fulfillment at God's appointed time?

Luke, the physician, one of the four Evangelists or Gospel—writers testified to his friend, a nobleman by the name of Theophilus, that he had made a careful investigation as to all these things, and gives in his record minute details which are conclusive and convincing.

The chosen vessel to carry out God's plan was a Jewish virgin by the name of Mary (Hebr. Miriam), who was of the lineage of King David, the last branch of his dynasty. When the angel Gabriel, God's messenger, appeared to her, she was greatly troubled and disturbed. He said to her:

"Fear not, Mary: for thou hast found favor with God. And behold, thou shalt conceive and bring forth a son, and shall call his name JESUS.

"Then said Mary unto the angel, How shall this be, seeing I know not a man?

"And the angel answered and said unto her, The Holy Spirit shall come upon thee, and the power of the Highest shall overshadow thee: therefore also that holy thing that shall be born of thee shall be called the Son of God." (Luke 1:30, 31, 34 and 35)

To reassure her, the angel used similar words as the ones spoken to Sarah when the birth of Isaac was announced to her. Then, the angel said: "Is anything too hard for the Lord?" he said, "With God nothing is impossible." Then, through the miracle of Isaac's birth the nation of Israel came into existence, here, by the miracle of the Virgin-birth the Saviour came into the world.

Disregarding the consequences, the criticism and reproach of those around her, this noble Jewish maiden submitted herself to the will of the Almighty, saying humbly:

"Behold, the handmaid of the Lord: be it unto me according to the will of the Lord." (Luke 1:38)

It is very important now to consider *the name* which the Redeemer was to bear upon His birth, namely *Yeshuah, Jesus.* The Apostle Paul declares:

"God . . . hath given Him a name which is above every name; That at the name of JESUS every knee should bow . . . and that every tongue should confess that Jesus Christ is Lord, to the glory of God the Father." (Phil. 2:9—11)

The angel who announced the birth of Jesus stressed the necessity of giving Him the name "Yeshuah" because of its meaning, namely, Saviour, Helper, Restorer. He said:

"Thou shalt call his name JESUS, for he shall save his people from their sins." (Matt. 1:21)

From this passage of Scripture it also appears that the promised Redeemer came in the first place to save from sin the people to whom He belonged "according to the flesh," the nation of Israel. The question arises: "why?" Surely not because of any preference or respect of persons. There was a special reason for it, namely, the unique position that nation occupies in the Old Testament economy.

The Lord had chosen Israel, the descendants of Abraham, to become a channel of blessing for the world. He entered into a special covenant with them and gave them a holy law which separated them from all other nations, He called Himself "their Shepherd," but the arch-enemy of God, Satan, whose only aim is to frustrate God's plans, brought it about that they went astray and became "lost sheep" who needed to be gathered back into the fold, to be saved. They became transgressors of the *Law,* covenant-breakers, and scripturally were considered *the most sinful people.*

Therefore by sending the Redeemer in the first place to the "lost sheep of the house of Israel" God proved that "where sin abounded, grace did much more abound," and when in the fulness of time God sent forth His Son," He put Him under the law, that He "might redeem them that were under the law," by fulfilling it and by paying the penalty for the transgressions of the people with His own blood.

"*. . . he took on him the seed of Abraham. Wherefore in all things it behooved him to be made like unto his brethren, that he might be a merciful and faithful high priest in things pertaining to God, to make reconciliation for the sins of the people.*" *(Hebr. 2:16, 17)*

He entered into "the holy place" into the very presence of God with His own blood, and "obtained eternal redemption for us." (See Hebr. 9:12)

The relationship between God and the other nations was an entirely different one, He was their Creator, He loved them, as stated in Deut. 33:3 where we read: "Yea, he loved the peoples" (Hebr. Amim, Nations) and in His great Plan of Salvation the whole world was included. The Prophet Isaiah foretold:

"*It is a light thing that thou shouldest be my servant to raise up the tribes of Judah, and to restore the preserved of Israel; I will also give thee for a light to the Gentiles, that thou mayest be my salvation unto the end of the earth.*" *(Isa. 49:6)*

There is no doubt that the name "Jesus" given to the Redeemer implies that He is *the Saviour of all mankind, of the whole human race.*

"For God so loved the WORLD, that He gave His only begotten Son, that WHOSOEVER believeth IN HIM should not perish, but have EVERLASTING LIFE." (John 3:16)

However, to make it possible for all sinners to be reconciled unto God, a new foundation had to be laid, a *New Covenant established.*

The Covenant between God and Israel was broken by them and thus their contact with Him was severed and Israel found themselves on the same level as the other nations of the earth. The re-establishment of Israel's fellowship with God could be accomplished only on an entirely different basis than by keeping Laws and ordinances — on the basis of *Grace,* free, unmerited Grace.

In this Covenant of Grace all nations could be included and the promise given to the patriarch Abraham could be fulfilled that all the families of the earth would have a share in the blessings of his posterity.

The New Covenant is described by the prophet Jeremiah as entirely different from the one made with the "fathers":

"This shall be the Covenant that I will make with the house of Israel; After those days, saith the Lord, I will put my law in their inward parts, and write in their hearts; and will be their God, and they shall be my people." (Jer. 31:33)

The Old Covenant was established through Moses, the faithful servant of Jehovah; the New Covenant was instituted by God's only begotten Son Whom He *gave* to be "the propitiation for the sins of the whole world." (I John 2:2)

". . . being in the form of God, (the Saviour) thought it not robbery to be equal with God: But . . . was made in the likeness of men and being found in fashion as a man, he became obedient unto death, even the death of the Cross." (Phil. 2:5—8)

He *voluntarily* laid down His life and shed His blood to obtain eternal Salvation for all who will believe in Him.

"No man taketh it from me, but I lay it down of myself. I have power to lay it down, and I have power to take it again. This commandment have I received of my Father. (John 10:18)

This was possible only because He was the incarnate Son of God, "God manifest in the flesh."

Yes,

"Without controversy great is the mystery of godliness:

"God was manifest in the flesh, justified in the Spirit, seen of angels, preached unto the Gentiles, believed on in the world, received up into Glory."
(1 Timothy 3:16)

THE EARTHLY MINISTRY
OF THE MESSIAH

The manifestation of God in the Person of the Lord Jesus has a dual aspect.

When we study the Scriptures concerning the life and work of the Messiah on earth, we must keep in mind both sides of His nature — the *divine* and the *human*.

The Lord Jesus manifested Himself as the eternal Son of God, Who was from everlasting "in the bosom of the Father," before the foundation of the earth was laid and Who is One with the Father. He repeatedly declared that he who sees Him sees the Father.

On the other hand, we hear Him calling Himself the Son of man, because in His outward appearance He was like any other man, He — the Apostle Paul declares —

". . . *being in the form of God thought it not robbery to be equal with God: but MADE HIMSELF OF NO REPUTATION and . . . was made IN THE LIKENESS OF MEN." (Phil. 2:6, 7)*

133

Before Jesus started His earthly ministry, God sent forth a herald, a messenger, to announce His advent to the people who were in those days anticipating the coming of the Messiah, in a special way.

Through the last of the Old Testament prophets, Malachi, the Lord foretold:

"Behold, I will send my messenger, and he shall prepare the way before Me: and the Lord, Whom ye seek, shall suddenly come to His temple, even the MESSENGER OF THE COVENANT, Whom ye delight in; behold, He shall come, saith the Lord of hosts." (Mal. 3:1)

The name of this herald was Jochannan, or John and he is known from Scripture as *John the Baptist.*

He was an unusual personality. Even his birth was unusual: his father, the priest Zacharias, and his mother Elisabeth, were advanced in age when the prospective birth of a son was announced to them.

The Angel Gabriel, who appeared to Zacharias while he was serving in the Temple, revealed to him the great mission his promised son was appointed to carry out, in fulfillment of prophecy about the time preceding the coming of the Messiah. He said, as we read in Luke 1:15–17

"He shall be great in the sight of the Lord . . . he shall be filled with the Holy Ghost . . . and many of the children of Israel shall he turn to the Lord their God.

"And he shall go before Him in the Spirit and power of Elias . . . to make ready a people prepared for the Lord." (See Malachi 4:5, 6)

Before John started to carry out his mission, God manifested Himself to him in the same way as in the days of old He revealed Himself to all His prophets:

"THE WORD OF GOD CAME UNTO JOHN, the son of Zacharias in the wilderness." (Luke 3:2)

Thus endued with authority from on high John boldly stepped out with his great message:

"Repent ye for the kingdom of heaven is at hand!" (Matthew 3:2)

convicting everyone in the multitude of people who came out to him to the banks of the river Jordan of his sins and wickedness and evildoing, without any respect of persons: publicans and soldiers, Pharisees

135

and Sadducees, leaders of the people who were proud of being "Abraham's seed" — he treated all of them alike, warning them of impending doom, stressing their need of repentance and "bringing forth fruits worthy of repentance."

He was that "voice in the wilderness" of which Isaiah declared that its task was to "make straight in the desert the highway for God." His awe-inspiring figure, his mighty voice made a great impression upon the masses who flocked around him day after day and they began to think that *he* was the awaited Messiah himself.

But he repudiated such thoughts by emphatically declaring:

"I am not the Christ . . . He it is Who coming after me, is preferred before me, Whose shoes latchet I am not worthy to unloose." (John 1:20, 27)

The multitudes who came out to John and listened to his message confessed their sins and were baptized by him in the Jordan.

Baptism was a religious ritual which symbolized sanctification and was performed by the high priest especially on "Yom Kippur", the Day of Atonement. The Hebrew term for baptism "Tvilah" means

136

"immersion". All proselytes had to undergo this ritual. Even today, when a Gentile embraces the Jewish faith he has to be immersed in a special basin containing fresh spring water; this is not simply a "washing" but it symbolizes death, burial and resurrection to a new life.

John was commissioned by God to baptize with water in order that the Messiah, Whom he himself did not know, should be manifested to Israel. (See John 1:31)

John was given a sign by which to recognize Him as he testifies:

"He that sent me to baptize with water, the same said unto me: Upon whom thou shalt see the Spirit descending, and remaining on him, the same is he which baptizeth with the Holy Ghost. And I saw and bare record that this is the Son of God." (*John 1:33, 34*)

This actually took place when Jesus came to John to be baptized, in order "to fulfill all righteousness" (as we find recorded in Matthew 3:13—15).

"And Jesus, when he was baptized, went up straightway out of the water: and lo, the heavens were opened unto him, and he saw the Spirit of God

137

descending like a dove, and lighting upon him:
"And lo a voice from heaven, saying, This is
my beloved Son, in whom I am well pleased." (Matt.
3:16, 17)

This was the first New Testament manifestation of the Deity, by which the Messiah was revealed to Israel as the Son of God.

Another special revelation was given to John the Baptist concerning Jesus:

"The next day John seeth Jesus coming unto
him, and saith, Behold, THE LAMB OF GOD, which
taketh away the sin of the world." (John 1:29)

To John the Baptist was allotted a great task; to him was given the privilege to be the immediate forerunner of the promised Messiah. He was "a burning and a shining light," and the Lord Jesus Himself bore testimony that "among those that are born of women there is not a greater prophet than John the Baptist: but he that is least in the kingdom of God is greater than he." *(Luke 7:28)*

This difference in greatness lies in the fact that with the coming of the Messiah "The *grace of God* that bringeth Salvation hath appeared to *all men."*
(Titus 2:11)

From then on free entrance into the Kingdom of heaven is obtained — not by *works* of righteousness, not by keeping the law, but only by "the faith of Jesus Christ." (Galatians 2:16)

After Jesus was baptized by John the Baptist in the river Jordan and *His Messiahship, His anointing,* had been revealed to the people by God's special proclamation and visible manifestation, He "was led up of the Spirit into the wilderness to be tempted of the devil", as we read in Matthew 4:1. Each one of the subtle onslaughts of the arch-deceiver of mankind was repelled by Jesus — using "the Sword of the Spirit, the Word of God." His mighty *"It is written!"* — caused the devil to leave Him.

However, this was only for *"a season"* as it is recorded by Luke. During the earthly ministry of the Lord Jesus, Satan returned time and time again to tempt Him, to divert Him from carrying out the purpose for which He came. "He was in all points tempted like as we are, yet without sin." (Heb. 4:15)

The record about the beginning of the public ministry of Jesus shows that He first of all proclaimed the same message as did John the Baptist:

"Repent: for the kingdom of heaven is at hand."

(Matt. 4:17)

He was the One Who had come to establish this Kingdom.

On a Sabbath day in the beginning of His ministry the Lord Jesus went to the synagogue of Nazareth and "stood up to read." He opened the book of Isaiah and what He read was the program outlined for the Messiah to fulfill.

"The Spirit of the Lord is upon me, because he hath anointed me to preach the gospel to the poor; he hath sent me to heal the brokenhearted, to preach deliverance to the captives, and recovering of sight to the blind, to set at liberty them that are bruised, To preach the acceptable year of the Lord. And he closed the book, and he gave it again to the minister, and sat down. And the eyes of all them that were in the synagogue were fastened on him. And he began to say unto them. This day is this scripture fulfilled in your ears. And all bare him witness and wondered at the gracious words which proceeded out of his mouth." (Luke 4:18–22a)

By that time "there went out a fame of him through all the region round about." He had started to carry out His Messianic program and His teaching

140

amazed all who listened to Him:

"*Never man spake like this man,*" (*John 7:46*) people were saying about Him,

"*. . . for he taught them as one having authority, and not as the Scribes.*"

Great multitudes from all parts of the Land followed him and they brought unto him all sick people that were taken with diverse diseases and torments, and those which were possessed with devils . . . and he healed them." (*Matt. 6:23*)

Thus He could justly declare in the Synagogue of Nazareth at the end of His reading of Isaiah's prophecy:

"*This day is this Scripture fulfilled in your ears.*" (*Luke 4:21*)

However, a careful study of this proclamation and other predictions concerning the reign of the Messiah, such as Isaiah 11:1—4 with its description of His attributes and characteristics and all His accomplishments — shows that these pertain to two different stages and that the carrying out of the Messianic program has *two phases,* of which the first one was fulfilled at the *first Advent of the Messiah* and the second one still *lies in the future.*

141

With this in mind, we can better appreciate the difficulties on the part of the people of Israel—their inability to recognize in Jesus the promised Messiah, especially in view of the circumstances in which the nation found itself at that period of its history.

From the very beginning of His public ministry the Lord Jesus repeatedly called the attention of those who surrounded Him and eagerly listened to His teaching that the kingdom He came to establish at that time was *of a spiritual nature.*

His "Sermon on the Mount" with its Beatitudes, His interpretation of the Law, emphasizing the spiritual side of it, the cleansing of the Temple, all His great works and miracles aroused interest on the part of the religious rulers of the Nation.

Nicodemus, who "came to Jesus by night," was a representative of those who recognized in Him "a teacher come from God" and the purpose of his visit was to find out if He was merely a great new teacher, or perhaps the promised Messiah Himself.

Immediately Jesus pointed out to Nicodemus that in order to understand Him and the purpose of His coming — in order to *see* the Kingdom of God, which He was proclaiming — *knowledge was not*

142

sufficient — a radical change of the whole human nature, a "new birth", had to take place:

"Verily, verily, (Amen, Amen) I say unto thee, Except a man be born again, he cannot see the kingdom of God." (John 3:3)

Marvel not that I said unto thee, Ye must be born again. (John 3:7)

To enter into the kingdom of God, to have eternal life, a man must be "born of the Spirit of God" and this is obtained through faith in the One Who came down from heaven as "the Son of man", but who was the eternal Son of God.

"For God so loved the world, that He gave His only begotten Son, that whosoever believeth in Him should not perish, but have everlasting life." (John 3:16)

Another cardinal truth about God was revealed by the Saviour to the Samaritan woman at the well of Sychar — the truth concerning the right way to worship God, He said to her:

"Woman, believe me, the hour cometh . . . and now is, when the true worshippers shall worship the Father in spirit and in truth; for the Father seeketh such to worship Him. (John 4:21 to 23)

A careful study of the Gospels not only shows that the teaching of the Lord Jesus was entirely different from the teaching of the Scribes, but that He brought an entirely new conception of God to the people — revealed Him in a new light: He spoke of Himself as being the personification of God, as being "One with the Father," as proclaiming only His Father's words and performing His Father's deeds. He gathered around Himself a select group of twelve disciples to whom He was able to reveal "the deeper things of God" and to whom He could entrust the Mission of spreading the "good Tidings."

"He ordained twelve, that they should be with Him, and that He might send them forth to preach, and to have power to heal sicknesses, and to cast out devils." (Mark 3:14, 15)

He was surrounded also by a greater group, who followed Him, but they did it only up to a certain point. The longer Jesus went about performing great signs and wonders, healing the sick, opening blind eyes and deaf ears, even raising the dead, the longer He was teaching in their synagogues and other places, always stressing the spiritual meaning and purpose of His coming, the more divided became the

144

opinion of the people about Him, and we read in the Gospel of John that after a very serious talk about a deep spiritual subject:

". . . *many of His disciples, when they had heard this, said, This is a hard saying; who can hear it?"* (John 6:60)

"From that time many of His disciples went back, and walked no more with Him." (John 6:66)

His devoted "twelve", however, continued to follow Jesus and even though they, too, could not fully comprehend His teaching, they wanted to stay with Him, to be near Him so when He asked them: after the others had left:

"Will ye also go away? Simon Peter answered Him, Lord, to whom shall we go? Thou hast the words of eternal life. And we believe and are sure thou art the Christ, the Son of the living God." (John 6:67—69)

On another occasion the Lord Jesus asked His disciples what people thought of Him and after hearing the different answers He put the question to them personally,

"But whom say YE that I am? And Simon Peter answered and said, Thou art the Christ, the Son of

145

God." (Matthew 16:15, 16)

This statement is one of the greatest declarations found in the New Testament concerning the Messiah, and it was not Peter's *own opinion.*

The Lord Jesus on hearing this solemn statement from Simon's lips, said:

"Blessed art thou, Simon Bar-jona: for flesh and blood hath not revealed it unto thee, but my Father which is in heaven." (Matt. 16:17)

In commemoration of this great revelation, Simon received a new name — "Peter" meaning "Rock". The Lord Jesus said:

Thou art Peter, and upon this rock I will build my church, and the gates of hell shall not prevail against it." (Matt. 16:18)

Peter's *declaration* was surely that "Rock" upon which the Church was built — a firm immovable foundation.

Peter himself had a long way to go yet, through many up's and down's in his spiritual life until he became the great Apostle as he is now known:

"From that time forth began Jesus to shew unto his disciples how that he must go unto Jerusalem, and suffer many things . . . and be killed,

146

and be raised again the third day." (Matt. 16:21)

This was such a perplexing statement that it was hard for the disciples to grasp its full significance. As usual, it was Simon Peter who acted as spokesman for them:

"Then Peter took Him, and began to rebuke Him, saying, Be it far from thee, Lord: this shall not be unto thee." (Matthew 16:22)

Saying this Peter again was only an "instrument" but this time it was the arch-deceiver who influenced him and the Lord Jesus immediately recognized Satan speaking through Peter and therefore reproved him sharply:

"Get thee behind me, Satan: thou art an offence unto me: for thou savourest not the things that be of God but those that be of men." (Matthew 16:23)

This was a solemn experience. The Lord had to prepare His disciples for the things which lay ahead, but it was too early yet to declare them openly and therefore

". . . charged He His disciples that they should tell no man that He was Jesus the Christ." (Matt. 16:20)

The expectations of the people, their hopes and

147

aspirations in connection with the coming of the Messiah were those of power and glory, political deliverance, the restoration of the throne of David, the setting up of an earthly kingdom.

They were unable to understand the words of Jesus:

"My Kingdom is not of this world" and His prediction about the necessity for the Messiah to suffer, to lay down His life, before He could enter into His glory.

How this reminds us of the solemn words of Isaiah at the beginning of his vision of the suffering Messiah, recorded in the 53rd chapter of his prophecy:

"Who hath believed our report, and to whom is the arm of the Lord revealed?"

MANIFESTATION ON THE
MT. OF TRANSFIGURATION

Peter's declaration: "Thou art the Christ, the Son of the living God," constituted a turning-point in the relationship between the Lord Jesus, the divine Master, and His disciples. From that time on He began to reveal to them what was going to take place in the near future and speak to them about the final outcome of His earthly ministry.

We do not know what transpired during the week following the discourse which the Lord Jesus had with His disciples on this solemn subject. But we read that:

". . . it came to pass about an eight days after these sayings, he (Jesus) took Peter and John and James, and went up into a mountain to pray.

"And as he prayed, the fashion of his countenance was altered, and his raiment was white and glistering. And, behold, there talked with him two men, which were Moses and Elias:

*"Who appeared in glory, and spake of his de-
cease which he should accomplish at Jerusalem."
(Luke 9:28—31)*

Peter, James and John were "taken aside"
from the other Apostles to become eye-witnesses
of the glory and majesty of Jesus. They were those
who later either themselves wrote a great part of the
New Testament Scriptures or through whose instru-
mentality same was written.

The disciples were disillusioned in their expectations by what their Master revealed to them.
They too — like the rest of the nation — were looking
forward to the restoration of the kingdom of Israel
and deliverance from the yoke of the Romans by the
Messiah, and they were grieved over what Jesus
told them about His coming rejection by the elders
and His being delivered into the hands of the Gentiles to be crucified.

They needed reassurance and God granted them
on the "holy mountain" a special manifestation of
the divine nature of Jesus, of His true Messiahship.

Moses, the giver of the Law and *Elijah* its fiery
defender, appeared before the eyes of the Apostles,
but they beheld Jesus surpassing them in glory and

150

splendor.

Peter was so deeply impressed by this manifestation of the glory of his beloved Master that he was ready to remain in that sacred place, and he said to Jesus:

"Master, it is good for us to be here: and let us make three tabernacles; one for thee, and one for Moses, and one for Elias: not knowing what he said." (Luke 9:33)

The record found in the Gospel according to Matthew describes how at the same moment a bright cloud overshadowed them and they heard God's voice from heaven declaring:

"This is my beloved Son, in whom I am well pleased; hear ye him." (Matt. 17:5)

This was a reaffirmation of God's declaration at the time when the Lord Jesus first appeared in public at the river Jordan, but this time the solemn admonition was added: *"hear ye him!"* In other words, take heed to what He is saying! Obey Him! . . .

When the disciples heard this voice they fell on their faces in great fear until the Lord came and touched them and bade them arise. And we read, that

When they had lifted up their eyes, they saw . . .

151

JESUS ONLY." (Matt. 17:8)

This great and glorious manifestation was intended for no one but the disciples and they were enjoined to keep it to themselves. As they came down from the mountain

"Jesus charged them saying: Tell the vision to no man, until the Son of man be risen again from the dead." (Matt. 17:8)

Of what immeasurable value this experience was to the apostles when they had to go out to the people to fulfill the purpose for which they were called by their Master, namely "that He might send them out to preach," we see from Peter's testimony found in his Second Epistle, wherein he says:

"We have not followed cunningly devised fables, when we made known unto you the power and coming of our Lord Jesus Christ, but were EYE-WITNESSES OF HIS MAJESTY. For he received from God the Father honor and glory, when there came such a voice to him from the excellent glory, This is my beloved Son, in whom I am well pleased. And this voice which came from heaven we heard." (II Peter 1:16—18)

The Apostle John also testifies:

152

"That which we have seen and heard declare we unto you, that ye also may have fellowship with us; and truly our fellowship is with the Father and with his Son Jesus Christ." (I John 1:3)

LAST STAGE OF THE
MESSIAH'S EARTHLY MINISTRY

After His glorious transfiguration, the Lord
Jesus led the three disciples who were with Him on
the "holy mount" down into the valley. There they
encountered an extremely difficult situation in which
the disciples who had been left behind found themselves. A boy tormented by an evil spirit was brought
to them by his desperate father, beseeching them to
cast out the demon, but they proved to be utterly
helpless. Then Jesus came and here again He manifested His divine power over Satan. The record is:

*"Jesus rebuked the unclean spirit, and healed
the child . . . "*

All He had to do was to command, and obedience
was secured: evil spirits released their victims,
blind eyes and deaf ears were opened, sickness and
weakness disappeared; when He rebuked the elements of nature, the heavy wind, the raging waters
"they ceased and there was calm"; He was victor

even over death itself:

"I am the resurrection and the life: He that be-lieveth in me, though he were dead, yet shall he live." (John 11:25)

He declared this at the tomb of Lazarus, whom He raised from the dead after he had been buried for four days.

However, the closer drew the time of the consummation of Jesus' earthly ministry, the more outspoken He became in explaining to His disciples what the final aim and purpose of His coming to earth was, the more detailed became His predictions of that which awaited Him.

The public admiration reached its climax. There in the valley at the foot of the Mount of Transfiguration "they were all amazed at the mighty power of God. But while they wondered every one at all things which Jesus did, he said unto His disciples:

"Let these sayings sink down into your ears: for the Son of man shall be delivered into the hands of men . . . " (See Luke 9:43–45)

From that time on Jesus "steadfastly set his face to go to Jerusalem", because "the time was come for him that he should be received up."

THE LORD'S TRIUMPHAL ENTRY
INTO JERUSALEM

The prophet Zechariah in his inspired vision, foresaw this event in minute detail. He foresaw a multitude following the Messiah, and called them to rejoice:

"Rejoice greatly, O daughter of Zion; shout, O daughter of Jerusalem; behold thy king cometh unto thee; he is just, and having salvation, lowly, and riding upon an ass, and upon a colt, the foal of an ass." (Zech. 8:9)

This prophecy found its literal fulfillment when the Lord Jesus, surrounded by His disciples, entered the gates of Jerusalem riding upon the colt of an ass.

But before this took place, Jesus found it necessary to warn His chosen twelve, so that they would not be "carried away" by the triumphant reception He would receive;

"Behold, we go up to Jerusalem, and all things that are written by the prophets concerning the Son of man shall be accomplished.

"For he shall be delivered unto the Gentiles, and shall be mocked, and spitefully entreated, and

156

spitted on.

"*And they shall scourge him, and put him to death: and the third day he shall rise again,*" but "*they understood none of these things; and this saying was hid from them . . .*" (*Luke 18:31—34*)

The disciples of Jesus were the first ones at the descent of the Mount of Olives and approaching Jerusalem to "rejoice and praise God with a loud voice for all the mighty works that they had seen, saying, Blessed be the King that cometh in the name of the Lord . . . " (Luke 18:37, 38) "And a very great multitude spread their garments in the way: others cut down branches from the trees, and strewed them in the way. And the multitude that went before, and that followed, cried, saying, Hosanna to the Son of David: Blessed is he that cometh in the name of the Lord: Hosanna in the highest." (Matt. 21:8, 9)

They were all, including the disciples, expecting Jesus to fulfill at that time their national hopes and aspirations, and were ready to proclaim Him their King, not realizing that first of all they needed Him as *Saviour and Redeemer from sin.* That is the reason why the Lord Jesus

"*When he was come near and beheld the city,*

WEPT OVER IT saying, If thou hadst known, even thou, at least in this thy day, the things which belong unto thy peace! but now they are hid from thine eyes." (Luke 19:41, 42)

He foresaw and foretold the impending ruin of "the holy city", the destruction of the Temple — the nation's pride — through a renewed invasion by their enemies:

". . . they shall not leave in thee one stone upon another; BECAUSE THOU KNEWEST NOT THE TIME OF THY VISITATION." (See Luke 19:43, 44)

They did not recognize in Jesus Christ the One Who at that time came to "save His people from their sins," to be "wounded for their transgressions and bruised for their iniquities," to "lay down His life for His sheep," to be the "Lamb of God, Who taketh away the sin of the world."

THE LAST SUPPER

It was the week before the feast of the Passover. People from all corners of the Land and from abroad were gathering in Jerusalem to commemorate the great deliverance from their bondage in Egypt — after which God had made a Covenant with them to

158

be His people to show forth His praises.

Now the days of the Old Covenant were coming to an end. The prophecy of Jeremiah about the time when God would establish a New Covenant with the house of Israel and with the house of Judah was about to be fulfilled. It was to be instituted by the promised Messiah, the Lord Jesus Christ, on the basis of *grace* and was to include every one who would believe in Him. The first Covenant was broken by the children of Israel. They thereby separated themselves from their God, Who had elevated them to such a high plane. By their unfaithfulness they brought themselves down to the level of the other nations. There was no further need to keep them separate from the rest of the world by the Law of Ordinances which they had violated, therefore God in His justice and righteousness broke down the "middle wall of partition" between Israel and the other nations, and in His New Covenant of Grace He included the whole world.

This the Nation of Israel did not realize, did not see. They were utterly ignorant concerning God's Plan of Salvation for all mankind. Their eyes were blinded, and the Bible calls it a "mystery." This

159

"blindness in part happened to Israel," the Apostle
Paul says, "until the fulness of the Gentiles be
come in," until these could be brought in to become
partakers of the blessings of Salvation according to
the promise which God had made to the partiarch
Abraham.

The Jewish people did not realize either that
the Plan of Salvation would involve *suffering* for the
Messiah. This was a mystery even to the prophets
themselves. The Apostle Peter writes in his First
Epistle that believers in the Messiah receive by
their faith the salvation of their souls, adding that
"of that salvation the prophets have enquired and
searched deligently,

"*. . . what manner of time the Spirit of Christ
which was in them did signify, when it testified
beforehand the SUFFERINGS OF CHRIST, and THE
GLORY THAT SHOULD FOLLOW.*" *(See I Peter
1:9—11)*

The closer the time of this predicted suffering
came the more the Lord Jesus devoted Himself to
His disciples to explain to them His relationship
with the Father and their relationship to Him, as we
find recorded in the Gospel of John particularly in

160

the 13th, 14th, 15 and 16th chapters.

The great high priestly prayer found in the 17th chapter of John reveals the heart of the Saviour as no other passage of Scripture does and it should rightly be called *"the Lord's prayer."*

The Lord thoroughly prepared His apostles for the events which were to bring His earthly ministry to an end, especially stressing the fact that He was going to lay down His life voluntarily:

"Therefore .doth my Father love me because I lay down my life . . . no man taketh it from me, but I lay it down of myself. I have power to lay it down, and I have power to take it again." (John 10:17, 18)

"Now" —we read in the 22nd chapter of the Gospel by Luke — "the feast of unleavened bread drew nigh, which is called the Passover," and the Lord Jesus said to His apostles, that He had a great desire to be in close fellowship with all of them around the passover table for the last time, He said:

"I have desired to eat this passover with you before I suffer: for I say unto you, I will not any more eat thereof, until it be fulfilled in the kingdom of God." (Luke 22:15, 16)

There in the privacy of the Upper room He taught

them the great lesson of humility by washing their feet, by serving them, and there He instituted that which we now call "The Lord's Supper."

"He took bread, and gave thanks, and brake it, and gave unto them saying, This is my body which is given for you: this do in remembrance of me.

"Likewise also the cup after supper saying, This cup is the NEW TESTAMENT in my blood, which is shed for you"

or as we find recorded in Matthew:

"This is my blood of the New Testament (or New Covenant) which is shed for many for the remission of sins." (See Matt. 26:26)

This was the last intimate communion between the Lord and His remaining eleven disciples. Judas Iscariot had already left; he went out into the night to perform his sinister act of betrayal, inspired by Satan himself.

Before they left the Upper room where the last supper was observed, the Lord Jesus said to His disciples:

"Hereafter I will not talk much with you: for the prince of this world cometh, and hath nothing in me. But that the world may know that I love the

*Father; and as the Father gave me commandment
even so I do. Arise, let us go hence."* (John 14:30,31)
*"And when they had sung a hymn they went out into
the Mount of Olives."*

There in the Garden of Gethsemane a new encounter with the arch-enemy Satan was awaiting the Redeemer, but He was ready to meet him.

GETHSEMANE

In our discussion of the various Manifestations of the Deity we have now reached one which is very solemn and most essential in the working out of God's plan of Salvation, namely the manifestation in the Garden of Gethsemane.

It is not incidental that when talking to His disciples about the approaching enemy, the Lord Jesus calls him "the prince of this world." He foresaw that at the last moment Satan would launch an onslaught upon Him and, using all the forces of darkness at his command, would try to hinder Him from carrying out His work of redemption.

When Jesus entered the Garden to renew His strength in prayer, Satan attacked Him with a great impact to force Him to abandon the fortress of obedience.

In the Garden of Eden the arch-deceiver suc-
ceeded in severing connection between God and
man by inclining the primal ancestors of mankind to
disobey their Creator, and thus

*". . . by one man's disobedience many were
made sinners,"* (Rom. 5:19)

*". . . As by one man sin entered into the world,
and death by sin; and so death passed upon all men
. . . "* (Rom. 5:12)

From the time of Adam's fall Satan became "the
prince of this world," and he was determined not to
lose this title, to retain his rulership over mankind
and keep the keys of Hades and of death in his
hands. How could he allow himself to be defeated,
and let Jesus' prediction become true:

*"Now is the judgment of this world: now shall
the prince of this world be cast out?"* (John 12:31)

Satan was determined to cause "the second
Adam" — who had remained faultless and sinless
throughout His entire earthly life — to fall. There
should not be found upon earth a perfect being
worthy to redeem human souls from the power of sin
and death. Satan's aim was to devaluate the price

which God had set for the redemption of the world. By causing Jesus to become disobedient, Satan would succeed in making the Redemption of mankind through the shedding of the Redeemer's blood upon the Cross impossible. On no account should Christ die as the Lamb of God; never should He be allowed to ascend Calvary's Cross. To prevent this by all means was what Satan aimed to achieve by his on-slaught on the Lord Jesus in Gethsemane.

The battle in the Garden of Gethsemane was so severe, so hard, that the Lord told His disciples; "My soul is exceeding sorrowful, even unto death." (Matt. 26:38) He actually fought with death. The evangelist Luke, as a physician describes the condition in which the Saviour found himself as deathly agony, because as he says:

"His sweat was as it were great drops of blood falling down to the ground." (Luke 22:44)

Three times the Lord Jesus returned to His place of prayer alone. His disciples, even the closest ones, Peter, James and John, were unable to stay awake and to pray, as He repeatedly asked them to do.

He fought His battle alone, but we read that an

angel from heaven appeared to strengthen Him, and He emerged from this battle victoriously. His words became true:

"The prince of this world cometh and hath nothing in me." (John 14:30)

It was not the will of the Father that the Lord Jesus should die in Gethsemane. There is a remarkable passage found in the Epistle to the Hebrews which sheds some light upon the great mystery of Gethsemane. It reads:

Christ *"in the days of His flesh, when he had offered up prayers and supplications with strong crying and tears unto him that was able to save him from death, and was heard . . . "* (Heb. 5:7)

The mystery of Gethsemane remains unsolved, and we do not dare to say anything beyond that which "is written:"

"The secret things belong unto the Lord our God." (Deut. 29:29)

Nevertheless, following our Lord to Calvary it is our duty to look into this solemn experience of the Saviour in the light which the Scriptures shed upon it.

How little we know about o b e d i e n c e! How

166

glibly we use this word! Jesus, our Lord, at the crucial hour in Gethsemane, taught us the greatest lesson of obedience by yielding unreservedly to the will of His Father. He prayed:

"Father, if thou be willing, remove this cup from me: nevertheless, NOT MY WILL, BUT THINE be done." (Luke 22:42)

He arose from the ground as victor over the powers of darkness, ready to meet His earthly enemies, ready to go to Calvary. He called His disciples who still were not aware of the gravity of the hour, and said to them:

"Behold, the hour is at hand, and the Son of man is betrayed into the hands of sinners, Rise, let us be going, behold, he is at hand that doth betray me." (Matt. 26:45, 46)

When Judas Iscariot with the band of men and officers which had been given to him by the chief priests and Pharisees, entered the Garden with lanterns, torches and weapons, Jesus, Whom Judas greeted with a kiss, stepped forward and simply asked:

"Whom seek ye?"

What He had just experienced in communion

167

with His Heavenly Father and the victory He had won over Satan, must have left such refulgence upon His countenance and His whole appearance was so majestic that when the Saviour told them He was Jesus of Nazareth for whom they were looking

"they went backward and fell to the ground"

and He had to repeat that He really was the one whom they have been sent to arrest. Then they took Jesus and bound Him, and led Him away. (See John 18:3—8 and 12, 13)

The Son of man was now "delivered into the hands of sinners," as He had predicted.

JESUS' TRIAL BEFORE THE
COURT OF THE HIGH PRIEST

The "Great Sabbath" preceding the Passover feast was approaching, and the chief priests, the Pharisees, the members of the Sanhedrin were anxious to try Jesus as soon as possible and to pronounce their sentence.

They assembled in the middle of the night in the palace of the high priest Annas, who asked Him about His disciples and about His doctrine. For over three years the Lord Jesus had spoken openly to the world and His teachings were known to everybody. This was neither the time nor the place to explain things, nor would He have found open ears for His words.

Then the chief priests and elders searched for witnesses against Jesus in order to put Him to death, "but found none." Only by the mouth of *false witnesses* were they enabled to accuse Him of blasphemy. Jesus had nothing to say to this, "He held His peace." But when the high priest arose and said unto Him:

"I adjure thee by the living God, that thou tell us whether thou art the Christ, the Son of God," then Jesus not only confirmed his words but solemnly declared before the entire Sanhedrin:

"I say unto you, Hereafter shall ye see the Son of man sitting on the right hand of power and coming in the clouds of heaven." (Matt. 26:63, 64) They did not need any further witnesses: by His own mouth He declared Himself to be equal to God. "The high priest rent his clothes, saying, He hath spoken blasphemy" and they sentenced Him to death.

However, they did not carry out that sentence according to the law of Moses, namely, by stoning. They could have done this without any interference on the part of the civil authorities — as was the case in the execution of the first martyr, Stephen, whom they likewise found guilty of blasphemy.

The question might arise: "Why did they not act as their religious law prescribed, as found in Leviticus 24:16?" There can be only one answer to this: the Redeemer had to suffer death upon the cross, to shed His blood for the sins of the world and both Jews and Gentiles had to take part in putting Him to death.

The Lord Jesus solemnly predicted:

"The Son of man shall be betrayed unto the chief priests and unto the scribes, and they shall condemn him to death, and shall deliver him to the Gentiles to mock, and to scourge and to crucify him. . . " (Matt. 20:18, 19)

This was literally fulfilled.

JESUS BEFORE PILATE

In order to deliver Jesus to the Roman Governor of Judea, Pontius Pilate for trial the high priests and elders had to give His case a political aspect.

They accused Him of "perverting the nation and forbidding to give tribute to Caesar, saying that He Himself is the Christ, a King." When asked by Pilate if He were really "the King of the Jews," Jesus affirmed it. Nevertheless, Pilate did not find any fault in Him, and as soon as he learned that Jesus belonged unto Herod's jurisdiction, he sent Him to Herod, who was exceedingly glad to see the man of whom he had heard many things. He hoped to fully satisfy his curiosity, and even to · see a miracle performed before his eyes. He questioned Jesus "in many words" as we read in Luke's record:

"But he answered him nothing." (See Luke 23:1-9)

Like the Court of the High Priest and like Pilate when they first brought Jesus before him, Herod could find no fault in Him. As the scribes and the elders had done earlier that night, so Herod now and Pilate later by the hands of their servants and soldiers beat Jesus and mocked Him, spat in His face, ill-treated Him in many ways, but were unable to find any guilt in Him for which they would have a judicial reason to put Him to death.

Clad in a fancy robe in mockery, the Saviour was then sent back to Pilate.

By that time — as Isaiah so vividly foresaw in his prophetic vision — "His visage (already) was so marred more than any man, and his form more than the sons of man." Especially after Pilate's soldiers had put a purple robe on His shoulders, pressed the crown of thorns upon His brow, and placed a reed to serve as a scepter in His tied hands, thus mockingly disguising Him as a king, Pilate presented Him to the people "who hid their faces from Him, despised Him, and esteemed Him not." (See Isa. 52:14 and 53:3) This was the crucial hour of the Messiah's rejection by His people.

The arrogant Roman Governor, who despised the people as well as their prisoner and did not want to have anything to do with them, entered then into the judgment hall and called Jesus for trial. There at Gabbatha the Son of man manifested Himself in such majesty, that Pilate could not help exclaiming: "Ecce Homo! Behold the man!" (John 19:5) With

dignity and authority Jesus answered all Pilate's
questions, and when Pilate, to sum up all his questioning of Jesus asked, *"ART THOU A KING
THEN?"* He delivered one of the greatest testimonies
concerning Himself:

*"Thou sayest that I am a king. To this end was
I born, and for this cause came I into the world, that
I should bear witness unto the truth, Every one that
is of the truth heareth my voice."* (John 18:37)

In passing, going back to the crowd which was
awaiting his decision — not expecting any answer,
Pilate asked "What is truth?"

Pilate found no guilt in Jesus, and he put the
final decision into the hands of the people. They
had already made their choice by asking him to release the robber Barabbas, not Jesus as Pilate suggested. But once more he tried:

"Behold your king," he said to them. But they
cried out: "Away with Him, crucify Him." Again
Pilate asked: "Shall I crucify your king?" but the
answer was: "We have no king but Caesar and they
put Pilate "on the spot" by saying: If thou let this
man go, thou are not Caesar's friend. Then he delivered Jesus to be crucified. (See John 19:14—16)

173

Although Pilate washed his hands to signify his innocence in the sentencing of Jesus, his action has gone down in history as judicial murder.

However, one very significant statement which the Lord Jesus made during His trial by Pilate should never be overlooked. After He had given Pilate a clear testimony about Himself, Jesus refused to answer any further questions:

"Then saith Pilate unto him, Speakest thou not unto me? Knowest thou not that I have power to crucify thee, and have power to release thee? Jesus answered: THOU COULDEST HAVE NO POWER AT ALL AGAINST ME, EXCEPT IT WERE GIVEN THEE FROM ABOVE." (John 19:10, 11)

Jesus denied Pilate's authority. He went to the Cross "despising its shame," because He chose to do so, in obedience to the perfect will of the Heavenly Father. He voluntarily ascended the Cross and "His own self bare our sins in his own body on the tree . . . " (I Peter 2:24)

174

CALVARY

The Glorification of the Saviour on the Cross

The purpose of the miraculous incarnation of the promised Messiah was to be the Saviour of mankind, "the Lamb of God, Who taketh away the sin of the world." (John 1:29) He came to lay down His life, to offer Himself for the remission of sin, to "pour out His soul unto death," according to the prophecy of Isaiah (53:12) "that through death He might destroy him that had the power of death, that is the devil." (Heb. 2:14)

His goal from the very beginning was *the Cross* and towards that goal His face was steadfastly set throughout His entire earthly life. Golgotha, the Cross of Calvary, was to be the altar on which the blood of the Lamb of God had to be shed, according to God's predetermined Plan of Salvation. *Golgotha was the "Moriah" of the Heavenly Father.*

However, we know from Jesus' own testimony given to His disciples and to His judges that He went to the Cross of His own accord, voluntarily, and He spoke of it as *His glorification*. In His prayer recorded in John 17 the Saviour says:

175

"Father, the hour is come, glorify thy Son, that thy Son also may glorify thee. . . " (John 17:1)

When Pilate delivered Jesus to be crucified, all the garments which were put on Him in mockery and derision were taken off and He went up to Calvary "in His own raiment." Pilate also ordered that an inscription be placed at the head of the cross: "Jesus of Nazareth, King of the Jews" — in Hebrew, Greek and Latin for everyone to read.

How erroneous it is to consider the crucifixion of Jesus as *His* tragedy! It surely was rather the *tragedy of Israel,* whose spiritual blindness prevented their recognizing in Jesus their Saviour and Redeemer. It was the tragedy of all mankind, as the apostles expressed it in their prayer found in the Book of Acts:

"For of a truth against thy holy child Jesus, whom thou hast anointed, both Herod, and Pontius Pilate, with the Gentiles, and the people of Israel, were gathered together. . . " (Acts 4:27)

The arch-deceiver did not give up his endeavors to prevent Jesus from dying upon the Cross. He tried to persuade Him to descend from it and to manifest His divine power by saving Himself as He had saved

176

others, thus proving that He really was the King of Israel and the Son of God. (Matt. 27:41—43)

The enemy used for that purpose the elders, the priests and the scribes, who promised to believe in Jesus if He came down from the cross but this was impossible, Satan's doom was sealed.

This was the hour when God's decree pronounced over Satan in the Garden of Eden was to be carried out "the head of the serpent shall be crushed." (lit. trans. Gen. 3:15)

The crucifixion of Jesus was a most awesome scene: The earth quaked and rocks were rent asunder, the sun "hid its face" and all was enveloped in darkness, but the face of the Saviour shone in heavenly light for the penitent malefactor whose prayer of faith was, "Lord, remember me when thou comest into thy kingdom." Jesus responded by promising:

"Verily I say unto thee, today shalt thou be with me in paradise." (Luke 23:42, 43)

The Roman Centurion who supervised the crucifixion was overwhelmed at the sight and "gave God the glory," saying: "Truly this man was the Son of God." (Matt. 27:56) Even the Jewish multitude returning from Calvary beat upon their breasts in penitence and remorse.

From the account of the four Evangelists we have a full detailed picture of the happenings on Calvary, and "the seven Words" of the Saviour uttered on the Cross have been most carefully preserved for us.

It was the hour of Judgment. Sin was being judged. *"He Who knew no sin" was "made sin" for all.* It was the hour when God's righteousness was fully satisfied and the love of God for humanity was manifested in fullest measure.

Only for a brief moment the Saviour felt forsaken by His Heavenly Father and exclaimed in a loud voice: Eli, Eli, lama sabachthani — My God, my God, why hast thou forsaken me?" (Matt. 27:46)

However, there could never be anything in the life of Jesus like that which happened to Job of old (as we read in the book bearing his name), namely, that He could be left in the hands of Satan for any length of time.

After He had uttered this cry, He immediately knew that

". . . *all things were NOW accomplished, that the Scripture might be fulfilled . . ."* and triumphantly exclaimed *"It is finished"* *(John 19:28, 30)*

"And when Jesus had cried with a loud voice, he said, Father into Thy hands I commend my Spirit: and having said thus, he gave up the ghost." *(Luke 23:46)*

At that moment — we read in the Gospel of Matthew:

"Behold, the veil of the Temple was rent in twain from the top to the bottom. . . " *(Matt. 27:51)*

"A new and living way" was now opened for all to enter into the very presence of God: by faith all can now "with boldness enter into the holiest by the blood of Jesus" and are encouraged to "draw near with a true heart in full assurance of faith." (See Heb. 10:19—22)

"Worthy is the Lamb that was slain to receive power, and riches, and wisdom, and strength, and honor, and glory and blessing." *(Rev. 5:12)*

THE RESURRECTION OF THE MESSIAH
"Christ is risen! — Christ is risen, indeed!"

This is the basic truth of the Gospel. If Christ had not risen from the dead His life, His sufferings, His death upon the Cross would all be futile; there

179

would be no "Good Tidings" to proclaim and all preaching would be in vain, as the Apostle Paul says in I Cor. 15:12—23, but with full assurance he proclaims that the message entrusted to him by the Lord Himself consists of facts which are beyond any shadow of doubt, namely, that

"Christ died for our sins according to the Scriptures; that he rose again the third day according to the Scriptures . . . " (I Cor. 15:3, 4)

God manifested Himself in the life of His only begotten Son as the Almighty, as the Omnipotent sovereign over life and death. "The Lord would not suffer His Holy One to see corruption." (Psalm 16:10) It was impossible for death to hold Him, because through His vicarious atoning death the Son of God "destroyed the one that had the power of death, that is the devil" and "death was swallowed up in victory."

The empty tomb is the greatest evidence, the most convincing proof of Jesus' Messiahship, of His deity.

For forty days the risen Redeemer manifested Himself "by many infallible proofs" as the *living One,* to various people and on different occasions

Hundreds of witnesses saw Him, had fellowship with Him, had the opportunity to hear Him speaking of the things pertaining to the Kingdom of God. (See Acts 1:3; I Cor. 15:5–8)

The apostles could therefore proclaim, later, with great authority

"This Jesus hath God raised up, whereof we all are WITNESSES" (Acts 2:32)

However, it took time for them to gain this glorious conviction. Following Jesus during the years of His public ministry, His disciples became more and more certain that at last the promised Messiah, the Saviour, the Restorer of Israel had come. They expected Him to manifest Himself as such at any moment, especially when He entered Jerusalem for the last time.

Despite His oft-repeated predictions concerning the outcome of His earthly ministry, despite His clear declaration that "the Son of man shall be delivered into the hands of men," that "He must suffer many things and be rejected of the elders and chief priests and scribes and be slain, and be raised the third day," we find it stated time and again in the Gospel records: *"they understood not this saying,* and it was hid from their eyes, and *they perceived it not.*" They could not grasp the meaning of their Master's agonizing supplication in Gethsemane and were unable to join with Him in prayer, but Jesus knew that this was the hour when the prophecy was to be fulfilled:

"I will smite the shepherd, and the sheep of the flock shall be scattered abroad." (Matt. 26:31) He told them so, and it actually came to pass.

None of them, except John, the beloved disciple, was present at the Lord's crucifixion. They hid themselves behind closed doors, filled with fear and apprehension. All their fond hopes and expectations had vanished since their Master was dead and buried. They could not believe the testimony of the faithful women who found the stone rolled away, the tomb empty, and to whom celestial beings announced that He was risen, neither believed they Mary Magdalene who had seen her beloved Master in person. The minds of the Apostles were darkened by disillusionment and disappointment and they were unable to believe.

Two of the disciples went the same day, when the Lord Jesus arose, to the village of Emmaus. It was quite a lengthy journey during which they naturally spoke about the things that had filled their souls with grief and sorrow, about the events that brought all their hopes and expectations to naught. Suddenly a "stranger" joined them — who asked them about the cause of their sadness, and who to their surprise seemingly knew nothing about the tragedy which had occurred in Jerusalem three days before.

They poured their hearts out to the sympathetic stranger and shared with him all their disillusionment and heartache. Then, in response to their complaints, He said unto them, "O fools and slow of heart to believe all that the prophets have spoken: Ought not Christ to have suffered these things, and to enter into His glory?" (Luke 24:25, 26)

"And beginning at Moses and all the prophets he expounded unto them in all the Scriptures the things concerning Himself." (Luke 24:27)
Because it was the risen Saviour Who had joined them on their way to Emmaus, but they did not recognize Him. Only their hearts "burned" within them while He talked with them by the way, and opened to them the Scriptures." They did not want to part

183

with Him and invited Him into their home for the night — then bade Him share their supper. At the table

"He took bread, and blessed it, and brake, and gave to them. And their eyes were opened, and they knew Him; and He vanished out of their sight." *(Luke 24:30, 31)*

The two disciples were so overwhelmed with joy that — disregarding their tiredness and the lateness of the hour — they immediately turned back to Jerusalem to take the good tidings to their despondent brethren who were still behind locked doors brooding over the sad happenings, although some of them confirmed that the Lord was risen indeed and appeared to Peter.

In spite of that it was as hard for them to believe these men, as it was to believe Mary Magdalene, who earlier had brought them the report that Jesus was alive. In both cases we read "they believed not . . . " So later, when the risen Lord appeared to His disillusioned disciples, we find in the record of Mark that "He upbraided them with their unbelief and hardness of heart, because they believed not them which had seen Him after He was risen."

184

(See Mark 16:9—14)

However, He showed them His love and for-
bearance in abundant measure, manifesting Himself
as "the One *Who was dead but is alive,*" giving them
tangible evidence of that fact. How patiently and
compassionately the Saviour treated His weak disciples!

According to the record of Luke, the Lord Jesus
stood in the midst of His disciples just as the men
from Emmaus finished their testimony, and greeted
them with the word: "Shalom" — "Peace be unto
you" — "But they were terrified and afraid and sup-
posed that they had seen a spirit." Lovingly He
asked them: "Why are you troubled? Why do thoughts
(or doubts) arise in your hearts? Behold my hands
and my feet, that it is I myself: *handle me* and see
. . . and he showed them his hands and his feet.
"And while they still disbelieved — but now because
they were overwhelmed with joy and wonderment —
the Lord gave them further evidence by asking for
food and eating it before their eyes.

Thomas was not present when the Lord appeared
for the first time to the other Apostles after His
resurrection.

Where had Thomas been? Had his faith in Jesus been so badly *shaken* that he had definitely deserted even the company of His disciples? — We find nothing in the Scriptures to explain the absence of Thomas, but that he was one of the most devoted of Jesus' disciples is evident from his expression: *"let us also go, that we may die with Him."* (*John 11:16*) when Jesus declared that He was going to Bethany, where their friend Lazarus had died. Thomas said that because the Jews had threatened to *stone Jesus* there.

Now he must have heard all the rumors about the Lord's body being stolen and other reports and he longed to know what had actually happened to the body of His beloved Master.

When he returned to his fellow-disciples he learned that they had seen the Lord — that He was *alive* — He had risen from the dead. Thomas wanted to see Him too, he wanted to be *sure* and he said to them: "Except I shall see in his hands the print of the nails and put my finger into the print of the nails and thrust my hand into his side, I will not believe." This statement earned for him the by-name "doubting Thomas." But was he really a doubter? Was there anything wrong with his desire to receive personal evidence on such an important matter as this and was he asking for anything more than the others had already experienced?

Furthermore, how could he conceive that the statement of his brethren was true, when they still — a week after the risen Saviour had appeared to them — were hiding behind locked doors? He could not understand why the Lord did not remain with them. Could it not be, after all, just an illusion on their part? The record is:

"Then came Jesus, the doors being shut, and stood in the midst, and said, "Peace be unto you!"

Without waiting for any utterance on the part of Thomas, He immediately responded to the longing of that apostle's heart, saying,

"Thomas, reach hither thy finger, and behold my hands; and reach hither thy hand, and thrust it into my side; and be not faithless, but believing."

Yes, Thomas, I want you to be sure that I am the same Jesus Whom you love. I want you to be fully convinced that I have actually risen from the dead that *I am alive.* This was the meaning of the Saviour's gentle offer. Did Thomas really touch His wounds?

Never! But he did something which none of the others had done, he fervently exclaimed:

"MY LORD AND MY GOD!" *(John 20:25—27)*

Could a man who was a doubter have done that so spontaneously and earnestly? To give such a testimony it takes a great character, a man of courage and deep sincerity.

It is true that the Lord Jesus said to him: "Thomas, because thou hast seen me, thou hast believed; blessed are they that have not seen and yet believed." But it is well to note that the Lord did not say this to Thomas at first, but only after inviting him to behold His wounds. Was this a rebuke, or was it rather a divine admonition, an injunction which concerned not only Thomas, but all followers of the Lord Jesus Christ?

The Lord Jesus did not remain with His disciples after His resurrection, but during forty days He appeared at various times in different places, manifesting Himself as the Living One to individuals and to groups of His followers — larger and smaller ones — to confirm the fact that everything God had spoken by the mouth of His holy prophets concerning the Messiah had found literal fulfillment in His

188

Person, life, ministry, death and resurrection from the dead. He also spoke to the apostles, as we find recorded by Luke in the 1st chapter of the Book of Acts, "of things pertaining to the Kingdom of God." because they were anticipating that *now* He would certainly "restore again the Kingdom of Israel." He explained to them that this was entirely dependent upon the counsel of His heavenly Father and would come to pass in the time and season which "the Father had put in His own power." It was not for them to know it.

What the risen Saviour expected them to do in the meanwhile was to be *His witnesses,* and especially to testify to the fact of His resurrection from the dead. *For that reason* "He showed himself alive after His passion by many infallible proofs" to various individuals and groups, as we stated before, so that their testimony would not be based upon heresay but upon their personal experience.

Among these we find Peter mentioned first, or at least separately from the other Apostles. There was a reason for this. A study of Peter's personality and nature shows how fervently he loved His Master but also how miserably he failed Him time and time again. His words in verse 3 of the first chapter of his first Epistle indicate what the resurrection of Jesus Christ meant to Peter personally and to every believer in the risen Lord. He writes:

"Blessed be the God and Father of our Lord Jesus Christ, who according to His abundant mercy hath begotten us again unto a living hope by the resurrection of Jesus Christ from the dead."

New life! A living hope! The risen Saviour manifested His forgiving love to Peter who had denied Him at the crucial hour of His trial by appearing to him apart from the other Apostles, and then at the Sea of Tiberias (or Sea of Galilee). He came to meet them as He had told Mary Magdalene and the other women on the resurrection-morning: "Go, tell my brethren that they go into Galilee, and there shall they see me." In this same message conveyed to the women by the Angel whom they met at the empty tomb, Peter is mentioned separately as we find recorded by Mark (16:1—8).

There, after a night of fishing when they "caught nothing," as we read in John 21:3 they saw Jesus standing on the shore, but did not recognize Him. He asked them tenderly, "Children, have ye any meat?" "No," was their reply, and when He told them what to do and the result was such an abundance of fishes that they were not able to draw in their net, John recognized the Lord and called Peter's attention to it, he immediately "cast himself into the sea." He wanted to reach the shore as soon as possible, in order to be close to his beloved Master.

A meal had already been prepared for the tired and hungry disciples, and a fire by which they could warm themselves, and the gentle voice of their Lord invited them, "Come and dine."

Then the remarkable conversation between the Lord Jesus and Peter took place which fully restored his apostleship:

"Simon, son of Jonas, lovest thou me?" the Lord asked Peter three times and each time Peter answered "Yes, Lord, thou knowest that I love thee." After each reply the Lord allotted a special task to Peter: "feed my sheep", "feed my lambs." The Good Shepherd Himself had accomplished His task, He Who "came to the lost sheep of the House of Israel" laid down His life for them and for "the other sheep" too, as He said: "other sheep I have also, which are not of this fold: them also I must bring, and they shall hear my voice; and there shall be one fold and one shepherd." (John 10:16) The risen Saviour commissioned Peter to be His under-shepherd to lead the straying sheep of the house of Israel back to "the Shepherd and Bishop of their souls."

THE LORD'S ASCENSION TO HEAVEN AND HIS COMMISSIONS TO THE APOSTLES

The great "mystery of godliness" of which the Apostle Paul speaks in I Timothy 3:16 consists not only in the fact of the miraculous incarnation of the Messiah — whereby "God was manifested in the flesh," but it was climaxed by the glorious ascension of the promised Messiah to Heaven. After His task upon the earth had been accomplished, He was "received up into glory."

In His high-priestly prayer the Lord Jesus said: "Father, the hour is come; glorify thy Son, that thy Son also may glorify thee . . . I have glorified thee on the earth; I have *finished* the work which thou gavest me to do. And now, O Father, glorify thou me with thine own self with the glory which I had with thee before the world was." (John 17:1,4 and 5)

God glorified His Son on the Cross: He also glorified Him by raising Him from the dead. All that had been predicted about the earthly ministry of the

Messiah was fulfilled. Now the time arrived for the great prophecy of David, the Psalmist, to find its fulfillment too. We find that prophecy in Psalm 110, wherein we read:

"The Lord said unto My Lord, Sit thou at My right hand, until I make thine enemies thy footstool." *(Ps. 110:1)*

A more literal rendering of the Hebrew text would be "Jehovah said unto my Lord, Sit thou at my right hand" —thus God is placing the Messiah as equal to Himself. Then the expression "sit" implies sitting down after an accomplished task. The Lord says to the Messiah (as it were) "Sit down after thou hast finished the work of Salvation, after thou hast suffered on the cross and shed thy precious blood as the price of sinner's redemption, after thou hast come forth from the tomb, come and sit at my right hand." It does not say forever, but "until I make thine enemies thy footstool." The Hebrew word "hadom" used here suggests "until thine enemies become silent in submission at thy feet.

In the meantime the disciples whom the Saviour had chosen "that they should be with Him, and that He might send them forth to preach . . . (Mark 3:14)

194

were to spread the "Good Tidings" about the finished work of the Messiah, *first* among their own people
and *then* in all the world.

The Lord Jesus started sending out His apostles
while He was still with them on earth, and his *first*
Commission to them was *"Go not* into the way of the
Gentiles, and into any city of the Samaritans enter
ye not: *But go* rather to the lost sheep of the house
of Israel. And as ye go, preach saying: The Kingdom of heaven is at hand." (Matt. 10:5—7)

He Himself came in the first place, to *Israel*
and untiringly and unceasingly He went about not
only preaching and teaching but "doing good" and
performing outstanding miracles. The disciples whom
He at that time had commissioned to go forth, two by
two, were to follow along the same line and not to
go to the Gentiles *then.*

In His *second commission,* given right after
His resurrection, the Lord gave His apostles the
authority, the purpose and the direction for their
ministry. He appeared to them as the Risen One,
greeting them with the words, "Peace be unto you!"
— embuing them with the Holy Spirit and saying:
"As My Father hath sent me, even so send I you."

(John 20:21) He was sent by the Heavenly Father to go primarily to the lost sheep of the house of Israel," — to that shepherdless people to win them back to the fold to which they really belonged.

From the Old Testament Scriptures we know how God identified Himself as "the Shepherd of Israel" and from the New Testament we see how Jesus called Himself "the Good Shepherd" who came to lay down His life for His sheep.

The *third Commission* which the Lord Jesus gave to His Apostles was probably the hardest one, namely, to be *witnesses* to the fact of His resurrection — in the city where He was sentenced to death by the Sanhedrin, the High Court and delivered by them to Pontius Pilate, the Roman Governor who carried out the sentence by crucifying Him. To go to *Jerusalem* where the people believed the tale which had been spread by the elders that the Apostles had stolen Jesus' body — was vitally important. His disciples were the only ones who as eye-witnesses could testify that the One Whom they had seen *alive* was the *same Jesus Whom they knew, the same one Who was rejected and crucified and buried in that well-guarded tomb.* They needed great courage for this task, great power from above, and the Lord promised:

"Ye SHALL RECEIVE POWER, after that the Holy Ghost is come upon you: and YE SHALL BE WITNESSES UNTO ME both in Jerusalem and in all Judea, and in Samaria, and unto the uttermost part of the earth." (Acts 1:8)

It is well to note that the Hebrew word "Aretz" translated as "earth" also means "land". "The land of Israel" needed to be covered by the testimony of these eye-witnesses before the Lord could give His last and greatest commission, viz. "Go ye into all the world and preach the Gospel to every creature. (Mark 16:15)

"So then after the Lord had spoken unto them, He was received up into heaven, and sat on the right hand of God." (Mark 16:19)

We find a more detailed account of the Lord's Ascension in Luke's report to his friend, Theophilus in the first chapter of the Book of Acts.

The last meeting of the Lord Jesus with His disciples took place on the Mount of Olives (or Olivet). Besides all the other things the Lord had spoken to them which we have already mentioned, the Commissions He gave them, the tasks He allotted to them, He gave them also the explicit command "not to depart from Jerusalem, but to wait for the promise of the Father" — of which He had spoken to them before, namely, the outpouring of the Holy Spirit. Only *then* would they be able to carry out their divinely appointed mission.

After their beloved Lord and Master had been received by a cloud out of their sight, they remained there for a while looking steadfastly toward heaven; the record is:

"Two men stood by them in white apparel, which also said, Ye men of Galilee, why stand ye gazing up into heaven? The same Jesus, which is taken up from you into heaven, shall so come in like manner as ye have seen Him go into heaven." (Acts 1:10, 11)

He did not depart forever. He will *come again* and all that was spoken by the mouth of God's holy prophets about the Messiah which did not come to pass at His first Advent, will be gloriously fulfilled.

MANIFESTATION OF THE LORD
JESUS TO THE HEAVENLY HOSTS

The Apostle Paul in his declaration about the great "mystery of Godliness" says that the manifestation of God in the flesh was "*seen of the angels.*" This is a very important thought.

Angels are "ministering spirits, "messengers of God; they are pure, sinless, celestial beings and their relationship to God is on an entirely different basis from that which exists between God and man.

The working out of God's great Plan of Salvation was something they could not comprehend, but could only observe with awe and admiration. The Apostle Peter speaking of the Gospel and what it means says, that *into these things* "*the angels desired to look . . .* " (See I Peter 1:10, 11)

Throughout the entire earthly ministry of the Saviour on every prominent occasion we find that the angels were present.

It was an angel who proclaimed the great

manifesto concerning the birth of the Saviour in Bethlehem:

". . . *Fear not: for, behold, I bring you good tidings of great joy, which shall be to all people. For unto you is born this day in the city of David a Saviour, which is Christ the Lord.*" *(Luke 2:10,11)* Then, there was with the Angel a multitude of the heavenly hosts, praising God and saying:

"*Glory to God in the highest, and on earth peace, good will toward men.*" *(Luke 2:14)*

Angels ministered unto Jesus in the wilderness after His first temptations by Satan; they strengthened Him at the time of His agony in Gethsemane.

Angels were the first witnesses to His resurrection from the dead and the first messengers to announce that event.

What a revelation of God's love it must have been for them to see the One Who was "equal with God" sitting at the right hand of the majesty on high" descend from heaven, to make Himself "of no reputation," to see Him "lower Himself to the extent of "taking on Himself the form of a servant," a human body of flesh and blood — to be exposed to the severest attacks and temptations by Satan, to suffer a cruel shameful death upon the Cross, because "God so loved the World that He gave His only begotten Son" to die for it and because the Son Himself was willing to lay down His life for fallen mankind.

What a manifestation of God's Grace and Mercy it was for the angels to see the Lamb of God shedding His pure, sinless blood on the Cross for the remission of the sins of humanity and by His death and glorious resurrection obtaining eternal Salvation for the posterity of Adam — who were "dead in trespasses and sins" opening "a new and living way" into the presence of God for "everyone who believeth, that he should not perish but have everlasting life." (John 3:16)

Every sinner saved, every "prodigal son" returning to his heavenly Father causes great rejoicing in heaven as the Lord Jesus declared in His parables recorded in St. Luke 15.

We can have only a very faint idea of the triumphant return of the victorious Redeemer to Heaven and the welcome which He received when He manifested Himself to the innumerable inhabitants of the celestial realm. We can hardly fathom what is described in Revelation 5:11, 12 but the words which conclude that passage and in which all the redeemed ones will join some day, are marvelous:

"Worthy is the Lamb that was slain to receive power, and riches and wisdom and strength, and honour, and glory and blessing."

MANIFESTATION OF THE DEITY
AS THE HOLY SPIRIT

Throughout the Bible we find the Holy Spirit mentioned in many passages not only in the New Testament, but on the pages of the Old Testament as well.

At the time when Elohim, the Almighty God, created heaven and earth

". . . the Spirit of God hovered above the waters."

as the Hebrew original of Genesis 1:2 should be rendered.

In the writings of the prophets the Spirit of God the Holy Spirit, is frequently mentioned not as a power or influence, but as a Person. We read in Isaiah 63:10 about the Holy Spirit that *he* was vexed or grieved because of Israel's rebellion.

The longing of all Old Testament saints is expressed in David the psalm-singer's prayer:

"Cast me not away from thy presence; and take not thy Holy Spirit from me." (Ps. 51:13)

203

The question arises: "Does the Christian faith in the Triunity of God have any basis in the Old Testament, or was it so deeply shrouded in mystery that no trace of it can be found?

As we have already mentioned in the Introduction to this study, the Sages of old who did not acknowledge Jesus Christ as the promised Messiah nevertheless believed in three distinct appearances of God: (1) as the Father, (2) as the "Shekinah Glory" visible to the high priest when he entered the Holy of Holies in the Sanctuary and to the people in the Cloud ascending from the Mercy Seat and resting over the Tabernacle, and (3) as the "Ruach Ha kodesh," the Holy Spirit.

These three revealments of the Deity are according to the teaching of the Sages united *in one.* And in their liturgic prayers, as well as in their daily worship, the Jewish people confess their belief in God, the Holy One, in the visible Shekinah and in the hidden Holy Spirit, which they consider as a *unity,* as one.

The term "Echod" as applied to the Deity strongly emphasizes this idea of *Unity,* otherwise the term "Yachid" would be used, meaning "soli-

204

tary one."

When Moses declared: "Hear ye nation of Israel Jehovah our God is One" he used the term "Echod."

In the New Testament, from the day of the Redeemer's miraculous incarnation till the day of His glorious ascension to heaven, we find God visibly manifested in the person of Jesus Christ, as God, *the Son.*

After His (the Lord's) ascension, the era of the Holy Spirit began; His universal Mission started.

Shortly before going to the cross of Calvary, where He was to accomplish the great work of redemption, the Lord Jesus revealed to His disciples the expediency and importance of His departure from the earth after His task was finished and Salvation had been brought forth for the whole human race for everyone who believes in Him. Unlimited by time or space the Holy Spirit will continue the working out of God's plan of Salvation upon the earth.

These are the words the Lord Jesus spoke to His disciples about the Holy Spirit:

". . . now I go my way to him that sent me . . . I tell you the truth: It is expedient for you that I go away; for if I go not away the Comforter will not

205

come unto you; but if I depart, I will send HIM unto you." *(John 16:5, 7)*

It is well to note that the Lord Jesus speaks of the Holy Spirit as a Person not a power or divine influence. His name is "The Comforter," as the name of God the Father is "Jehovah" and the name of God the Son "Jesus" (Hebr. Yeshuah—*Saviour)*

The Lord Jesus also gave His disciples an outline of the program the Holy Spirit was to carry out, He would first of all:

"reprove the world of sin, and of righteousness, and of judgment: Of SIN (the Lord Jesus said) because THEY BELIEVE NOT ON ME: of RIGHTEOUS-NESS, because I go to my Father, and ye see me no more; of JUDGMENT, because the PRINCE OF THIS WORLD IS JUDGED. (John 16:8—13)

Besides that, the Lord explained:

"I have yet many things to say unto you, but ye cannot bear them now, Howbeit, when HE, the Spirit of truth, is come, he will guide you into all truth." *(John 16:12)*

". . . the Comforter, which is the Holy Ghost whom the Father will send in my name, he shall teach you all things, and bring all things to your

remembrance, whatsoever I have said unto you.''
(John 14:26)

All that the Lord said to His disciples concerning the Holy Spirit climaxes in the last promise which He gave them, in the last words He spoke on earth before He ascended to heaven:

''. . . ye shall receive power after that the Holy Ghost is come upon you, and ye shall be witnesses unto me . . . '' (Acts 1:8)

Fifty days after the resurrection from the dead, ten days after His ascension, that promise was fulfilled — the outpouring of the Holy Spirit took place.

It was a visible manifestation — just as at the river Jordan after Jesus was baptized the Holy Spirit appeared in visible form as a dove, so now "cloven tongues like as of fire" descended upon the heads of the believers, who obeying the Lord's injunction had remained in Jerusalem waiting in "the upper room" for "the promise of the Father."

What a mighty manifestation this was! The testimony of the Spirit-filled Peter moved the hearts of 3000 people to repentance and they accepted Jesus as their Saviour and Lord. The signs and wonders which the Holy Spirit enabled the Apostles to perform,

207

along with their powerful witnessing, caused another crowd of about 5000 men to become believers in the Saviour a few days later, and we read in the Book of Acts:

"And believers were the more added to the Lord, multitudes both of men and women." (Acts 5:14)

"And the Lord added to the Church daily such as should be saved." (Acts 2:47)

"And the word of God increased; and the number of the disciples multiplied in Jerusalem GREATLY; and a great company of the priests were obedient to to the faith." (Acts 6:7)

All of these were born again by the *Holy Spirit* and became the first-fruits of the New Covenant from among those who according to Old Testament law assembled in Jerusalem to celebrate "Shevuoth", the Feast of the first-fruits. They also were the first stones in the new *spiritual temple*, of which Jesus Christ is "the foundation and Chief Corner Stone."

THE LORD'S MANIFESTATION
TO SAUL OF TARSUS

It is well known that the Lord Jesus chose twelve men to be His Apostles, most of them being plain unlearned men. They were with Him throughout His earthly ministry. He was their Master, their Teacher, and they had the opportunity of sitting at His feet, as it were, daily, learning from the lips of the One Whose teaching amazed the lawyers and scribes of the Nation's hierarchy, not to speak of the multitudes who followed Him. Even at the age of twelve when He was sitting in the temple amidst the doctors, both hearing them and asking them questions — all that heard Him were astonished at His understanding and answers. The result of these men being with their divine Master all this time was clearly noticeable in their own ministry after His ascension to heaven. We read in Acts 4:13 as follows:

". . . *when they saw the boldness of Peter and John, and perceived that they were unlearned and*

*ignorant men, they marvelled; and they took know-
ledge of them THAT THEY HAD BEEN WITH JESUS."*

Twelve men, according to the number of the
tribes of Israel, trained and prepared by their Heavenly Teacher to be "His witnesses" — witnesses to
His life, to His crucifixion and to His glorious resurrection from the dead primarily among their own
people; to those He appeared after His resurrection
and with them He fellowshipped for 40 days.

One of them was lost, Judas Iscariot, who betrayed Him, but this too — like everything else in
the life of the Messiah was in order that "the Scripture might be fulfilled."

Another had to be chosen in Judas' place —
one who could qualify for the task allotted to him,
namely, to be a *witness* for the Lord. It had to be a
man, who had companied with the apostles *all* the
time that the Lord Jesus went in and out among
them, beginning with His baptism by John unto that
same day that He was taken up from them. Only such
a person could be ordained to be, together with the
other Apostles, a "witness to the Lord's resurrection." (See Acts 1:22)

Of the two men who were equally so qualified,

210

the Apostles, after earnest prayer to God Who knows the hearts of all men, chose Matthias upon whom the lot which they had cast fell, and he was numbered with the eleven Apostles, and was present with them at the time of the outpouring of the Holy Spirit.

It was most essential and important, as we have already indicated, that the testimony concerning the bodily resurrection of the crucified Saviour should be given all over the land of Israel by *eyewitnesses* to this fact. And that is what the Apostles, endued with the power of the Holy Spirit did with great effectiveness and marvellous results, as we pointed out in the previous chapter.

This stirred up the leaders of the Nation more than ever before. They tried to refute, to deny, the fact of Jesus' resurrection by spreading a rumor that the Apostles had stolen His body but this was of no avail.

Realizing their failure, the elders of the Nation organized a punitive campaign against those who confessed faith in the Lord Jesus. Great persecution caused the believers to leave Jerusalem and many of them, except the Apostles, were scattered abroad throughout the regions of Judea and Samaria. Some even left the country.

At the head of this punitive campaign was a young man by the name of Saul, who was from the city of Tarsus but had received his religious education in Jerusalem, at the feet of the great Rabbi Gamaliel. He was a Pharisee, who strictly observed the Law and had a great zeal for God, but like the rest of Israel's leaders, he did not know anything about God's Plan of Salvation. Saul was sure that he was performing a God-pleasing task when "entering into every house and hailing men and women, he committed them to prison." In his blind zeal without knowledge, Saul was "breathing out threatenings and slaughter against the disciples of the Lord," whom he considered as apostates, because the Church in those days consisted *exclusively* of Jewish *believers*.

After completing his "work" in Jerusalem, where he "made havoc of the Church," Saul decided to go to Damascus. With credentials from the high priests to present to the leaders of the synagogues he intended to seek out all the followers of Christ whether they were men or women, that he might bring them bound unto Jerusalem. (See Acts 9:1,2)

212

This man, this fiery defender of God's cause who in his blind zeal actually did not know what he was doing, was — as we find plainly stated in Acts 9:16 — "God's chosen vessel" and the Lord had in mind to accomplish great things through him.

The Manifestation of the Lord to Saul of Tarsus on the road to Damascus is one of the most impressive events recorded in the Scriptures. Saul and his companions were walking along the road approaching the city of Damascus. It was noon-time when a "light from heaven above the brightness of the sun shone round about them and they all fell to the ground." A voice from heaven called him twice by his name: "Saul, Saul . . . " Thus God spoke in the days of old to Abraham, to Moses, to Jacob, pronouncing their names twice. This was a sign to Saul that he was really hearing a divine voice, and the words which followed "cut him to the quick" — "Why persecutest thou me?" All he could say in reply was "Who art thou, Lord?" He was shocked and utterly perplexed. "I am Jesus whom thou persecutest," was the Saviour's simple response, — He gave him just His name "Yeshuah"; not "the promised Messiah", or any other title because He well knew that everything Saul had done was done through *ignorance*. The Lord Jesus showed the same compassionate love to Saul of Tarsus, as He manifested towards those who actually crucified Him — for whom He prayed while upon the cross, saying: "Father forgive them; for they know not what they do." (Luke 23:34)

Saul realized his ominous mistake and yielded his life unreservedly to the same Jesus Whom he had so fiercely persecuted before.

"Lord, what wilt thou have me to do?" (Acts 9:6) he asked immediately, ready to do whatsoever the Lord commanded him. This became the motto of his life; from that day on Saul, who was known later as the Apostle Paul, had no other ambition, no other desire, than to carry out the will of his Saviour Jesus Christ, Whose free-will bond-slave he became.

Saul arose from the ground a blind helpless man, who had to be led to Damascus by the hand, but he was an entirely new person — a humble, praying man, awaiting further instructions from his Lord and Master.

Such a momentous climactic conversion! Ananias, the disciple whom the Lord sent to Saul could hardly believe it possible that such a great change should have taken place in Saul and he was reluctant to go, but the Lord revealed to him His plans concerning Saul and Ananias went to him, as a messenger of the Lord, to restore his sight and to baptize him — after which Saul was filled with the Holy Spirit and "straightway he preached Christ in the synagogues that He is the Son of God." (Acts 9:20)

Moreover, by the infinite grace of God, Saul of Tarsus, Paul the Apostle, was able to join the company of *eye-witnesses* to the fact of the bodily resurrection of the Lord Jesus from the dead, because what he experienced on the road to Damascus was not just seeing *a vision* — the risen Saviour appeared to him *in person*.

In I Corinthians 15:8—10 the Apostle Paul, after enumerating all those by whom Jesus Christ had been seen after rising from the dead, testified:

"And last of all he was seen of me also, as of one born out of due time. For I am the least of the Apostles, that am not meet (worthy) to be called an Apostle, because I persecuted the Church of God. But by the grace of God I am what I am; and His grace, which was bestowed upon me, was not in

vain . . . "

The Apostle Paul occupies a unique position among those whom the Lord Jesus had chosen to continue His work upon the earth and his "commission" was a different one from the others. He was chosen "to bear the name of the Lord Jesus before the Gentiles and Kings, and the children of Israel" (Acts 9:15)

His background was different from that of the other Apostles. He was a highly educated man, able to meet the various groups and classes of people whom he approached with the Gospel-message upon their own ground. Paul was well-equipped to deal with rabbinical scholars as well as with Greek philosophers. He could appear before kings and rulers, in synagogues and in market-places, in the Temple and on Mars Hill, but wherever he went and no matter with whom he dealt, his was an uncompromising testimony; wherever he went the theme of his message was *"Christ the Crucified,* the power of God and the wisdom of God." Paul presented the Messianic claims of Jesus to his brethren after the flesh and proclaimed God's great plan of Salvation by grace both to Jews and to Gentiles, "not counting the cost." The ministry entrusted to Paul was the ministry of the New Covenant. He made a clear distinction between "the ministry of the letter," as he calls the Old Testament economy, and "the ministry of the Spirit."

Great revelations were given to Paul: great mysteries were disclosed to him, the greatest of which was

THE MYSTERY OF THE CHURCH

Saul of Tarsus was chosen and appointed by the Lord Jesus to be the Apostle to the Gentiles. That *Gentiles* could be partakers of the same blessings as the children of Israel, that they could be included in the commonwealth of Israel without first becoming proselytes, without being put under the "yoke" of the Law of Moses, was something entirely new even to the Council of the Apostles in Jerusalem. The Gospel which Paul preached was entrusted to him by a special revelation as he testified to the Galatians:

"... I *certify you, brethren, that the Gospel which was preached of me is not after man. For I neither received it of man, neither was I taught it,*

217

but by the revelation of Jesus Christ." (Gal. 1:11,12)

He was fully aware of the fact that he was God's chosen vessel to "preach His Son among the heathen," and therefore he laid aside immediately all his own conceptions and opinions; he did not "confer with flesh and blood;" he did not go to Jerusalem to the other Apostles, but went for a while into seclusion in the desert of Arabia to be alone with the Lord, and there he must have received his enlightenment, his instruction, so that later he could say: ". . . I received of the Lord that which I delivered unto you." It remains unknown how much time he spent in Arabia; but three years after he returned to Damascus, Paul went to Jerusalem and had fellowship with Peter for about two weeks and also met James, the Lord's brother.

After this brief visit the Apostle Paul resumed his traveling and everywhere he went he preached the Gospel of Christ to Jews and to Gentiles alike.

It is well-known that after the death of the first martyr Stephen durihg the persecution instigated by the Jewish hierarchy in which Saul of Tarsus in his blind zeal took such an active part, the believers were scattered abroad and settled in various parts of the then known world. In those places of their dispersion Churches were established which in the beginning consisted exclusively of Jewish believers. Even the Church in Antioch—where the followers of Christ for the first time were called "Christians"—was established by believers from among the Jews, as we read in Acts 11:19—21:

"Now they which were scattered abroad ... traveled as far as Phenice, and Cyprus, and Antioch, preaching the word to NONE BUT UNTO THE JEWS ONLY. And some of them were men of Cyprus and Cyrene, which, when they were come to Antioch, spoke unto the Grecians, preaching the Lord Jesus. And the hand of the Lord was with them: and a great number believed, and turned unto the Lord."

Those Grecians were not Gentiles but Hellenists or Grecian Jews, who had adopted the teachings of the Jewish philosopher Philo of Alexandria.

The Samaritans to whom Philip preached prior to Saul's conversion were not Gentiles either, as is evident from the conversation of the Lord Jesus with the Samaritan woman at the well of Sychar. She called the patriarch Jacob "her father"; she and her people were waiting for the coming of the

219

Messiah. Those of the ten tribes who returned from the Assyrian captivity under the leadership of Ezra and Nehemiah settled in Samaria, as it was from there that they had been taken into captivity. They had no fellowship with the Jews because of the political and also the religious separation which Jeroboam, the son of Nebat, brought about after the death of Solomon. (See I Kings, chapter 12)

Evidently it pleased the Lord to delay the ingathering of "the other sheep" of which the Lord Jesus spoke in John 10:16 as being "not of this fold," until Churches would be established to which — according to the divine plan — Gentiles could be added. It was not the Lord's intention to have separate churches for Jews and for Gentiles: on the contrary, His desire was that "there should be one fold, and one Shepherd."

It was one of the important points in the great "mystery of Godliness" revealed to Paul that God, Who was "manifested in the flesh" was to be "preached to the Gentiles." As a result of this preaching a new order was to be established. The New Covenant of Grace — which according to God's predetermined plan should include all nations — was to come into force, and the Gentiles were now to become partakers in the blessings of Abraham.

In his Epistles to the Romans, Paul emphasized the fact that Abraham believed God and *that* was counted unto him for righteousness — not his works. SALVATION by GRACE, and GRACE ALONE — excluding "works" — was one of the great revelations given to Paul and was one of the strongest points in his teaching: "No man can be justified by keeping the Law of Ordinances, therefore all believers are children of God by *faith in Christ Jesus.*"

"There is neither Jew nor Greek, there is is neither bond nor free, there is neither male nor female; for ye are all one in Christ Jesus." the Apostle Paul writes to the Galatians. To the Ephesians he declares:

". . . by Grace ye are saved through faith; and that not of yourselves: it is the gift of God: not of yourselves: it is the gift of God: not of works, lest any man should boast." (Eph. 2:8, 9)

It had already been revealed to Peter that as pertaining to Salvation the Lord "put no difference between the Jews and the Gentiles, purifying their hearts by faith." This lesson Peter learned when

221

he was sent to Cornelius, who was a God-fearing man, a centurion of the Italian band. By the means of a special vision repeated three times the Lord made it clear to Peter not to consider the other nations as unclean.

Therefore when after fourteen years of successful preaching among the Gentiles Paul returned to Jerusalem with his companion Barnabas and testified before the Council of the Apostles the great things which the Lord had wrought through their ministry, it was Peter who became their advocate and confirmed the fact that it was the Lord's will that the Gospel of Salvation should be preached to the Gentiles. It was he who brought forth this very important argument which put an end to the serious dispute concerning the necessity for Gentiles to observe the law of Moses.

"Peter rose up, and said unto them, Men and brethren, ye know that ... God made choice among us, that the Gentiles by my mouth should hear the Word of the Gospel and believe. And God, which knoweth the hearts, bare them witness, giving them the Holy Ghost, even as he did unto us; and put no difference between us and them, purifying their

hearts by faith. Now therefore why tempt ye God, to put a yoke upon the neck of the disciples, which neither our fathers nor we were able to bear? But we believe that through the grace of the Lord Jesus Christ we shall be saved, even as they." (Acts 15:7—11)

In his Epistle to the Ephesians the Apostle Paul especially magnified his apostleship to the Gentiles, considering it as a gift of God's Grace that to him was made known the mystery which in other ages was not made known unto the sons of men "that the Gentiles should be fellow-heirs (with the Jews) and *of the same body* and partakers of his promise in Christ." (see Ephesians 3:1—6)

By comparison with the human body and the relationship between husband and wife, the Apostle Paul explains the mysterious union between Christ and the believers who constitute His Church, His Body, His Bride, those whom He had redeemed "out of every kindred, and tongue, and people and nation," whom He loved and for whom He gave Himself,

"That he might present it to himself a glorious church, not having a spot, or wrinkle, or any such thing; but that it should be holy and without blemish."

223

(Eph. 5:27)

THE MYSTERY OF ISRAEL'S BLINDNESS

In connection with the mystery of the Church and the ingathering of the Gentiles, another mystery was revealed to the Apostle Paul, namely, "the mystery of Israel's blindness." Ever so often the question is asked: "Why did the Jewish nation reject Jesus as their Messiah?" and nobody gives a clearer answer to this question than the Apostle Paul.

We have previously pointed out the fact that the sin of Israel as a nation against Jesus was a "Shegaga", an act committed unknowingly, in ignorance. The loving Saviour, the everlasting High Priest, therefore disregarded their cry "His blood be upon us and upon our children" and in the last hour of His agony upon the Cross covered it by His compassionate intercession:

"Father, forgive them: for they know not what they do."

The Apostle Peter on the Day of Pentecost, when setting so vividly before the eyes of the Jewish nation their sin in rejecting and crucifying Jesus, emphatically states:

"I know, brethren, that you did it through IGNORANCE, as did also your rulers." *(Acts 3:17)* Peter did not tell them that they had crucified the Messiah—it was "Jesus of Nazareth" Whom they rejected; this was the reason, too, that when the Lord appeared to Saul of Tarsus on the road to Damascus He spoke of Himself using only His name:

"I am JESUS Whom thou persecutest." *(Acts 9:5)* The Apostle Paul says about the people of Israel ". . . had they known, they would not have rejected the Lord of glory." (I Cor. 2:8)

On His way to the cross the Lord Jesus wept over the tragic state of His people saying:

"If thou hadst known . . . at least in this thy day, the things which belong unto thy peace! but now they are hid from thine eyes." *(Luke 19:41, 42)*

Dealing with the subject of Israel's blindness, the Apostle Paul calls it "a mystery," saying: "I would not, brethren, that ye should be ignorant of this mystery, lest ye should be wise in your own conceits; that blindness in part is happened to Israel until the fulness of the Gentiles be come in." (Romans 11:25)

When the Apostle Paul visualized the mystery

225

of Israel's blindness in connection with Calvary, he did not consider it as a punishment; he gives glory to God and exclaims; "O the depth of the riches both of the wisdom and knowledge of God! how unsearchable are his judgments, and his ways past finding out!" (Rom. 11:33)

Israel's downfall as a Nation served as an opportunity for the Gentiles to obtain Salvation. "Salvation is of the Jews" the Lord Jesus declared, and through their stumbling it was made available to the rest of the world.

It is well to note that all of this was foreseen and predicted by God's holy prophets, as we read:

"Surely the Lord God will do nothing but He revealeth his secret unto his servants the prophets." (Amos 3:7)

And speaking of Israel's blindness the Apostle Paul refers to the prophecy of Isaiah found in the 29th chapter of his book:

"For the Lord hath poured out upon you the spirit of deep sleep, and hath closed your eyes: the prophets and your rulers, the seers hath he covered. And the vision of all is become unto you as the words of a book that is sealed, which men deliver to

one that is learned, saying, Read this, I pray thee:
and he saith, I cannot; for it is sealed: And the book
is delivered to him that is not learned, saying, Read
this, I pray thee: and he saith, I am not learned."
(Isa. 29:10—12)

However, this blindness is not to be permanent,
"God, forbid!" says Paul, answering the question:
"Have they stumbled that they should fall?" and
strongly emphasizes the fact that God has *not* cast
away His people — that "after the fulness of the
Gentiles be come in" a great and glorious future is
awaiting God's chosen people, who remain such because "the gifts and calling of God are without
repentence." (Rom. 11:29)

The Apostle Paul, writing to the Gentile Christians at Rome and stressing the fact that he "magni-
fies his office as the Apostle to the Gentiles," gives
them earnest admonitions in regard to their attitude
towards Israel and warns them not to think that the
Jews have forfeited forever their former position in
the sight of God. A careful study of Romans chapters
9, 10 and 11 would enlighten every Christian, even
today as to the place which Israel occupies in the
working out of God's Plan of Salvation and how the

227

other nations are made partakers of the same.

Using the analogy of an olive tree of which some branches were broken off and replaced by branches of a wild olive tree, the Apostle Paul seriously exhorts the Gentile Christians:

"Boast not against the branches ... well; because of unbelief they were broken off, and thou standest by faith ... Behold therefore the goodness and severity of God: on them which fell, severity; but toward thee, goodness, if thou continue in his goodness: otherwise thou also shalt be cut off. And they also, if they abide not still in unbelief, shall be graffed in: for God is able to graff them in again." (Rom. 11:18—23)

Israel's fate has not been sealed. Israel has a future, a glorious future. The divine promise made to Abraham that his posterity will become a blessing to the nations of the world still awaits fulfillment. The Apostle Paul says that after the fullness of the Gentiles shall come in:

"ALL ISRAEL SHALL BE SAVED." (Rom. 11:26)

"Now if the fall of them be the riches of the world, and the diminishing of them the riches of the

Gentiles; how much more their fullness . . . "

*"For if the casting away of them be the recon-
ciling of the world, what shall the receiving of them
be, but life from the dead?"* (Rom. 11:12, 15)

Paul did not wish that his Gentile brethren
should be ignorant of the mystery of Israel's blindness. He wanted them to have full understanding of
the situation and admonishes them at the end of his
discourse:

*"For as ye in times past have not believed God,
yet have now obtained mercy through their (Israel's)
unbelief: even so have these also now not believed,
that through your mercy they also may obtain mercy."*
(Rom. 30, 31)

FUTURE MANIFESTATIONS

Not *all* the predictions by God's holy prophets concerning the Messiah found their fulfillment in the earthly life and ministry of the Lord Jesus Christ. Many great things which God revealed to them are still awaiting realization.

The Apostle Peter calls the attention of the believers to the *prophetic word,* telling them that first of all they should know that "no prophecy of the Scripture is of any private interpretation. For the prophecy came not in old time by the will of man: but holy men of God spake as they were moved by the Holy Ghost." It is "a sure word," Peter says, and the believers "do well that they take heed unto it, as unto a light that shineth in a dark place, until the dawn and the day-star arise in their hearts." II Peter 1:19–21) Thus he is pointing them to the future which would reveal great and glorious things.

It is well to note that these future events in which God will manifest Himself pertain to the destiny of Israel as a nation in her relationship to God and His promised Messiah, on the one hand, and to the destiny of the Church of Jesus Christ, "His body," "His Bride" — on the other hand.

We have already considered the prophecies about the first Advent of the Messiah, His virgin birth, His ministry, His vicarious atoning death, His resurrection from the dead, and ascension to heaven, and we stated that all of these prophecies found literal fulfillment. This proves the verity of Peter's statement about the prophetic word and guarantees the fulfillment of everything that is predicted for the future.

Let us consider first of all:

THE RETURN OF THE MESSIAH TO ISRAEL

The prophets clearly foresaw that the Messiah at His first Advent when he would appear in the form of the humble servant of the Lord, as the Man of Sorrows, to suffer and to die, to "be cut off" — not for Himself but to bear the transgression of the people — would be rejected by the spiritually benighted Israel nation, as they would not recognize in Him "the Prince of Glory."

However, they just as clearly predicted that the time would come when "the arm of the Lord" of which the prophet Isaiah spoke in the 53rd chapter of his prophecy would be revealed to the nation of Israel and the Lord "would pour upon the house of David, and upon the inhabitants of Jerusalem the Spirit of grace and of supplications . . . " which would cause them to long for the coming of the Messiah, actually for His return. This is described by the prophet Zechariah in the remarkable prediction found in his chapter 12 verses 10—14.

Ever since the days when the Lord Jesus uttered this solemn lamentation over the nation of Israel and their holy city:

"O Jerusalem, Jerusalem, thou that killest thy prophets, and stonest them which are sent unto thee, how often would I have gathered thy children together, even as a hen gathereth her chickens under her wings, and ye would not! Behold, your house is left unto you desolate.

"For I say unto you, Ye shall not see ME henceforth, till YE shall say, Blessed is he that cometh in the Name of the Lord." (Matt. 23:37—39) —
ever since that serious warning was pronounced

232

and the solemn prophecy of Daniel concerning the destruction of the Sanctuary, confirmed by this prediction of the Lord Jesus, was actually and literally fulfilled,—the longing for the coming of the Messiah, (for His return) has become more and more an integral part of the spiritual life of the orthodox Jew. It found its expression in his prayers, his worship services, his confession of faith — although he does not realize that he is expressing a supplication for the coming *again of the same One Whom his nation had rejected!*

We could fill many pages with quotations from the Orthodox prayer-book confirming the above statement.

Every Jewish congregation when singing on the eve of the Sabbath the famous hymn "Lecha-Dodi" is using such impressive words as:

"Shake thyself from the dust, Arise, put on the garments of the Glory, O my people! Through the Son of Jesse, the Bethlehemite; draw thou nigh unto my soul; redeem it." *

In the most solemn portion of the Prayer-Book

---

* Daily Prayer Book of the United Hebrew Congregation of the British Empire with a new translation by Rev. S. Singer. New York Hebrew Publishing Company. Page 112.

233

for the Day of Atonement (Yom Kippur) we find a public confession reading as follows:

"Our righteous anointed is departed from us: horror hath seized us, and we have none to justify us. He hath borne the yoke of our iniquities, and our transgression, and is wounded because of our transgression. He beareth our sins on his shoulder, that he may find pardon for our iniquities. We shall be healed by his wound, at the time that the Eternal will create him (the Messiah) as a new creature. O bring him up from the circle of the earth. Raise him up from Seir, to assemble us the second time on Mount Lebanon, by the hand of Yinnon."*

(This word "Yinnon" is applied to the Messiah)

In that same Prayer-Book we find also the following portion for the Congregation to recite:

"He is our God; he is our Father; he is our King; he is our Saviour; he will save us and redeem us a second time; and he of his mercy will let us hear a second time, in the presence of all living. Behold I have redeemed ye in the latter end, as I have done at first, to be to you for a God. I am the Lord your God."*

* Mahzor Abodat Israel. Prayers for the Day of Atonement. Hebrew Publishing Company. 77—79 Delancy St., New York. Page 239.

234

The Messiah after accomplishing the work of redemption — which was the objective of His first coming — returned to heaven according to the prophecy of Hosea:

"I will go and return to my place, till they acknowledge their offence, and seek my face: in their affliction they will seek me early." (*Hosea 5:15*)
In other words, in compliance with His own prediction, the nation of Israel will not see the Lord Jesus again until they shall be ready to accept Him as their Saviour.

This time is vividly described in the prophecy in the 12th chapter of the Book of Zechariah which reads as follows:

"And I will pour upon the House of David, and upon the inhabitants of Jerusalem, the spirit of grace and of supplications: and they shall look upon me whom they have pierced, and they shall mourn for him, as one mourneth for his only son, and shall be in bitterness for him, as one that is in bitterness for his firstborn.

"In that day there shall be a great mourning ..." (*Zech. 12:10, 11a*)
This "mourning" the prophet compares with the

national lamentation over the death of King Josiah who was slain by the Egyptians in the valley of Megiddo (See II Chron. 35:23–27)

The spirit of grace of which the prophet speaks that it shall be poured upon Israel (a more accurate rendering would be "the spirit of *favor*" "Ruach Chein") will make them realize what they caused the Messiah to endure and it will be an individual mourning — the house of David, the prophets, the priests separately from each other and separately from their wives, will confess the gross error on their part to have rejected Him and they will supplicate and plead with God to send the Messiah, the pierced One, again. They will really long for His *return*.

And according to a further prediction by the same prophet Zechariah there will be a gracious response on the part of the Messiah to His lamenting people:

"In that day there shall be a fountain opened to the house of David and to the inhabitants of Jerusalem for sin and for uncleanness ..." (Zech. 13:1) "The fountain of water and blood which flowed from the pierced side of the Saviour upon the cross

of Calvary" — a fountain of Redemption and Cleansing for all — had to be opened before the Saviour could appear in Glory (for the second time) and reveal Himself to the waiting people as the Same One Whom they did not recognize at His first advent.

The Pierced One will answer the prayer of His mourning people and will descend upon the same spot from which He was taken up to heaven:

"His feet shall stand in that day upon the Mount of Olives." (Zech. 14:4)

Then He will manifest Himself not only as Saviour, as His name "Yeshuah" implies, but as Restorer, which is also one of the meanings of His Name.

At the hour of His ascension, when the Apostles asked Him: "Lord wilt thou at this time restore the kingdom of Israel? the Lord Jesus replied

". . . It is not for you to know the times or the seasons, which the Father hath put in his own power." (Acts 1:7)

It is well to notice that while the Apostles spoke of "this time", the Lord Jesus spoke of "times and seasons" which the Heavenly Father has outlined in His plan.

Before the final restoration of Israel as a nation can take place, before the second phase of the mission assigned to the Messiah can be worked out, a parenthetical time was appointed by the Father. This was to be used for *witnessing* among Israel to the fact of Jesus' resurrection — which was the most valid and conclusive proof of His Messiahship — and for carrying out of the great *"Go ye"* — *commission* to *preach* the Gospel in all the world, expressed by the Saviour as follows:

"All power is given unto me in heaven and in earth. Go ye therefore, and teach all nations, baptizing them in the name of the Father and of the Son, and of the Holy Ghost. Teaching them to observe all things whatsoever I have commanded you: and, lo, I am with you alway, even unto the end of the world. Amen." (Matt. 28:18—20)

This period was appointed — as before stated — for the ingathering of "the other sheep," who did not belong to Israel's fold and for the establishment of the Church.

THE LORD'S APPEARING FOR THE CHURCH

Two terms are used in the New Testament Scrip-

238

tures concerning the Second Coming of Christ:

(1) The Appearing of the Lord in glory

(2) The Return of the Lord or His coming again. These two expressions are of great significance and importance.

It is obvious that the term *"Return"* implies that there has been a first coming, whereas "Appearing" can only be said about an event which takes place for the first time.

At His first Advent the Lord Jesus came to "His own", to "the lost sheep of the house of Israel," and *to them* as a Nation He will *return,* whereas for the Church, for His redeemed ones" out of every kindred, and tongue, and people, and nation, the children of Israel who believe in Him included — it will be "a *glorious appearing.*"

In the second chapter of his Epistle to Titus the Apostle Paul speaks of the two aspects — the Lord's first coming and its purpose and also of His second Advent:

"For the grace of God that bringeth salvation hath appeared to all men, teaching us that, denying ungodliness and worldly lusts, we should live sober- ly, righteously, and godly, in this present world:

Looking for that blessed hope, and the glorious appearing of the great God and our Saviour Jesus Christ; Who gave Himself for us, that He might redeem us from all iniquity, and purify unto Himself a peculiar people, zealous of good works. (Titus 2:11—14)

What a glorious manifestation that will be!

THE RAPTURE

Among other truths and mysteries revealed to the Apostle Paul the mystery of the Rapture occupies a most important place.

A careful study of his Epistles to the Thessalonians reveals that the young Christians of the Apostolic era, who had to endure persecution and tribulations of many kinds, were wondering why the Lord Jesus did not come to deliver them out of their afflictions.

To those believers the Apostle Paul explained that afflictions and sufferings are inevitable in the life of Christians, and that "no man should be moved by them." "We told you before," he says, "that we should suffer tribulation." However, as he goes on in his writing, Paul makes it very clear that there are two kinds of tribulation — one which is aimed to test and strengthen the faith of the believer, while the other, which is called the "great tribulation," is described in Scripture as "the wrath of God" which is to come in retribution or as a punishment for unbelief. No Christian will ever have to suffer *that*, because Salvation in Christ, by Christ, delivers the believer from divine wrath, and the Apostle Paul assures the Thessalonians:

"God hath NOT appointed us to wrath, but to obtain salvation by our Lord Jesus Christ, Who died for us, that whether we wake or sleep, we should live together with him." (I Thess. 5:9, 10)

As far as the other trials are concerned, these should be patiently endured in view of the "blessed hope" of the Coming of the Lord, as we read in I Thess. 3:13:

"To the end he (the Lord) may establish your hearts unblamable in holiness before God, even our Father, at the coming of our Lord Jesus Christ..."

It is apparent from Paul's writings to the Thessalonian believers that they were deeply concerned about "the Rapture" which he described to them in vivid colors in the 4th chapter of his First Epistle wherein we read:

". . . the Lord himself shall descend from heaven with a shout, with the voice of the archangel, and with the trump of God: and the dead in Christ shall rise first: then we which are alive and remain shall be caught up together with them in the clouds, to meet the Lord in the air: and so shall we ever be with the Lord. Wherefore comfort one another with these words." (I Thess. 4:16—18)

Another detailed description of the Rapture is found in Paul's First Epistle to the Corinthians, as follows:

"Behold, I shew you a mystery; we shall not all sleep, but we shall all be changed, in a moment, in the twinkling of an eye, at the last trump: for the trumpet shall sound, and the dead shall be raised incorruptible, and we shall be CHANGED. For this corruptible must put on incorruption, and this mortal must put on immortality." (I Cor. 15:51—53)

The early Christians were expecting the Rapture to take place at any time especially in view of the many trials which they had to endure. But Paul's admonition was "to study to be quiet," to go about their daily business and not to be carried away by rumors, not to be "soon shaken in mind, or be troubled,

242

neither by spirit, nor by word, nor by letter as from us, as that the day of Christ is at hand." (II Thess. 2:2)

There must have been much confusion among the believers of that time concerning the second coming of Christ, causing the Apostles to admonish the believers to remain steadfast and *sober*, "putting on the breastplate of faith and love, and for a helmet, the hope of salvation" — according to the Lord's own injunction "to occupy till He comes."

We find the same thoughts expressed in the writings of the Apostle Peter who had to deal with another problem different from that of Paul, but not less disturbing to the minds of the young Christians. There had appeared among them scoffers, who denied even the possibility of the Lord's coming again. They said: "Where is the promise of His coming? For since the fathers fell asleep, all things continue as they were from the beginning of the creation." (II Peter 3:4)

About such scoffers the Apostle Peter says, that they will be overtaken by the "day of God" suddenly and unexpectedly, because it will come upon them as "a thief in the night," just as the

243

Apostle Paul explained to the Thessalonians, that only for unbelievers "the day of the Lord so cometh as a thief in the night. For when they shall say Peace and safety, then sudden destruction cometh upon them . . . but ye, brethren, are not of darkness, that that day should overtake you as a thief." (I Thess. 5:2—4)

Both Apostles give the believers practical advice. Peter reminds them that they have "the sure word of prophecy," whereunto they do well to take heed as unto a light that shineth in a dark place, until the day dawn and the day-star arise in their hearts." (II Peter 1:9)

Because they are fully aware that "the day of the Lord" will inevitably come when "the heavens shall pass away ... the elements shall melt with fervent heat, and the earth ... be burned up," and because they believe in the establishment of "new heavens and a new earth, wherein dwelleth righteousness," according to the Lord's promise, the Christian should be especially diligent to be found by the Lord at His coming "in peace, without spot, and blameless." (II Peter 3:14)

They should not consider the delay in His

appearing as "slackness" on His part, but as "long-suffering, because the Lord is not willing that any should perish, but that all should come to repentance." The Apostle Peter concludes his admonition by saying:

"Ye therefore, beloved, seeing ye know these things before, beware lest ye also, being led away with the error of the wicked, fall from your own steadfastness. But grow in grace, and in the knowledge of our Lord and Saviour Jesus Christ. To Him be glory now and forever, Amen." (II Peter 3:17, 18)

There is not much difference in this aspect between our day and age and the time of the Apostles. We find the same eager anticipation on the part of the believers — the same desire to be delivered from the trials and tribulations of the present state of world affairs by the appearing of the Lord in the clouds — to "be caught up in the Rapture and so be with Him forever."

There is also much confusion and controversy among the believers today concerning the different stages of our Lord's *Second Advent*, about the great tribulation, about the time of the Rapture, the establishment of the millennial Kingdom, and other matters which occupy the minds of Christians at present.

It is not our intention to deal with such controversies. Our aim is to present the various manifestations of the Lord as indicated throughout the entire Bible, and just briefly to mention some of these manifestations which are still to be expected in the future.

The Apostle Paul writes to the Thessalonian believers about "that man of sin," the son of perdition, who opposeth and exalteth himself above all that is called God, or that is worshipped; so that he as God sitteth in the Temple of God, showing himself that he is God." That is the Antichrist who according to the writings of the Apostle John denies that Jesus is the Christ, denies the Father and the Son. Although not revealed yet in person, he has had his adherents throughout the entire history of the Church. The Apostle Paul, speaking of his time says: The mystery of iniquity doth already work" and it is still working in the world today.

However, "the Wicked One" cannot be revealed in his full power until that which is restraining him will be removed or taken away from this earth. His prey are those who "do not believe the truth but have pleasure in unrighteousness." (II Thess. 2:12) The activity of the Antichrist according to Paul's statement is "after the working of Satan with all power and signs and wonders" which falsehood can devise. His reign is described in the Book of Revelation as most terrible. It is no wonder that time and time again great tyrants, despots and dictators were thought to be the Antichrist. It started with the Emperor Nero as the letters of his name (being also numbers at the same time) amount to the "number 666" known as the number of the Antichrist." (See Rev. 13:18)

But we, as Christians today, are not waiting for the Antichrist — we are looking forward to "the glorious appearing of our Lord and Saviour Jesus Christ."

Eventually the Lord will by a mighty manifestation of His power put an end to the reign of "that Wicked one." He will "consume him with the spirit of His mouth, and shall destroy him with the brightness of His coming." (II Thess. 2:8)

The Lord will establish His millennial Kingdom. The "second phase" of His ministry, predicted by

247

God's holy prophets, will find its fulfillment. He will return to His people and restore the throne of David. In remorse for their ominous mistake of the past, His people will accept Him as their Saviour and Redeemer, as predicted by the prophet Zecharaiah. (See Zech. 12:10)

The prophecy of Isaiah which is so well-known concerning "the Child" that was to be born, the Son Who would be given, Whose name is Wonderful, Councelor, The mighty God, the everlasting Father, the Prince of Peace, will be completely fulfilled, in its second portion as well, which reads:

"Of the increase of his government and peace there shall be no end, upon the throne of David and upon his kingdom, to order it and to establish it with judgment and with justice from henceforth even forever. The zeal of the Lord of hosts will perform this. (Isa. 9:7)

Under His reign there will be perfect peace for the whole creation, as we find this so vividly described by the prophet Isaiah in his 11th chapter verses 1–9. This picture of "the Kingdom of Peace" concludes with the statement that

"They shall not hurt nor destroy in all my holy

248

mountain: for the earth shall be full of the knowledge of the LORD as the waters cover the sea." (Isa. 11:9)

The promise given to Abraham about his posterity becoming "a blessing to all families of the earth" will find its fulfillment, when it shall come to pass that

". . . the mountain of the LORD'S house shall be established . . . and shall be exalted above the hills; and ALL NATIONS SHALL FLOW INTO IT. And many people shall go and say, Come ye, and let us go up to the mountain of the LORD, to the house of the God of Jacob; and he will teach us of his ways, and we will walk in his paths; for out of Zion shall go forth the law, and the word of the LORD from Jerusalem." (See Isaiah 2:1—3)

The future lies in God's hands. We can be certain that just as all the prophecies concerning the first Advent of the Saviour and His earthly ministry found literal fulfillment, so all the future manifestations foretold in God's Holy Word — the Second Coming of Christ, the Rapture, and everything that is included in God's great plan, will be fulfilled in His own good time. So, as Christians, we should be "looking for that blessed hope, the glorious appearing of the great God and our Saviour Jesus Christ" — not for our sake but for the sake of His glory.

The greatest comfort for every Christian is to be found in the parting words of the Saviour to His disciples:

"In the world ye shall have tribulation: but be of good cheer; I have overcome the world."

and in the statement of the Apostle Paul:

"Our conversation is in heaven; from whence also we look for the Saviour, the Lord Jesus Christ: Who shall change our vile body, that it may be fashioned like unto His glorious body, according to the working whereby He is able even to subdue all things unto himself." (Phil. 3:20, 21)